Driven to]

**A Case for
Inspector Morse**

from the ITV series

Screenplay
by **Anthony Minghella**

based on characters
created by Colin Dexter

edited by Linda Buckle

CAMBRIDGE
UNIVERSITY PRESS

Published by the Press Syndicate of the University of Cambridge
The Pitt Building, Trumpington Street, Cambridge CB2 1RP
40 West 20th Street, New York, NY 10011-4211, USA
10 Stamford Road, Oakleigh, Melbourne 3166, Australia

First published 1994

Printed in Great Britain at the University Press, Cambridge

A catalogue record for this book is available from the British Library

Minghella, Anthony.
Inspector Morse: driven to distraction: a screenplay / by
Anthony Minghella; based on characters created by Colin Dexter.
    p.   cm.
ISBN 0 521 46984 8 (pbk.)
1. Morse, Inspector (Fictitious character) – Drama. 2. Police – England – Oxford –
Drama. [1. Mystery and detective plays. 2. Plays.] I. Dexter, Colin. II. Title.
III. Title: Driven to distraction.
PR6063.I475157   1994
822'.914 – dc20   94–5032   CIP

ISBN 0 521 46984 8

The Inspector Morse drama *Driven to Distraction* was produced by Zenith Productions
for Central Independent Television and is based on characters created by Colin Dexter.

A number of Inspector Morse books written by Colin Dexter are available, published
by Pan Macmillan Ltd.

Last Bus to Woodstock
Last Seen Wearing
The Silent World of Nicholas Quinn
Service of All The Dead
The Dead of Jericho
The Riddle of The Third Mile
The Secret of Annexe 3
The Wench is Dead
The Jewel That Was Ours
The Way Through The Woods
Morse's Greatest Mystery and Other Stories

A videocassette of this film is also available to schools and colleges from the publishers.
Please contact:

Education Department
Cambridge University Press
The Edinburgh Building
Shaftesbury Road
Cambridge CB2 2RU

Contents

Introduction

The Morse novels by Colin Dexter and their subsequent adaptation for television are very much a part of the detective genre. Unlike mystery stories which emphasise the emotional effects of crime and the build-up of tension for the reader, detective novels concentrate on the nature of detection and the solving of a puzzle. Because of this the central character of the detective becomes all-important.

Modern-day detectives are still formed from a distinct pattern which can be traced back directly to Arthur Conan Doyle's creation, Sherlock Holmes. Sherlock Holmes is presented as a strong individual, who is a disturbingly eccentric loner, and highly intelligent with a keen interest in psychology and motivation. He is also identifiably British. Many, if not all, of these characteristics can be found in subsequent successful and popular detectives, most of whom have been translated very effectively onto television. Miss Marple, Lord Peter Wimsey, Poirot (albeit from Belgium), Dalgliesh, Wexford, Morse and, more recently, Jane Tennison of *Prime Suspect* and Fitz in *Cracker*, follow the strong pattern set by Conan Doyle. To offset their professional invincibility these detectives are often presented as privately lonely figures. The obsessive nature of detective work causes difficulties in relating to others, awkward or non-existent marriages, and emotional isolation. The main agent of detection does not need to be a member of the police force. Those that are (like Morse, Wexford, Taggart and Spender) are presented as mavericks – brilliant but with their own unorthodox and sometimes questionable methods. Miss Marple, Sherlock Holmes, Poirot and Peter Wimsey are amateur sleuths sought after for their abilities. All these detectives have in common their acute perception and ability to reach the truth, though their foibles may differ. Although they all have a reputation for intelligence which others find intimidating, this intellect is often hidden or disguised, a device used by authors to manipulate both plot and character, as well as adding an element of amusement for the reader or viewer. Miss Marple's appearance as a prim little old lady gives her a disguise from which to view and then surprise the world. This is also true for

Wexford with his grey, scruffy suit, and his ordinariness, and Morse with his social gaucheness, his drinking, and his reclusive lifestyle. Both Sherlock Holmes and Morse have their assistants. Dr Watson and Sergeant Lewis highlight the genius of their superiors, as well as possessing personal and detecting qualities of their own. Lewis is portrayed as being more conventional and also more human than Morse. There is no doubt that the development of their relationship is central to all Morse films, and the interaction of personality and method make them a formidable team.

Authors use the detective genre as a vehicle for exploring the inner crevices of human lives and relationships. In some respects the reader or viewer is put in the same position as the detective, needing to be alert and perceptive. But unlike life there are comforting rules to this fiction. We know the clues are there and that the truth will be revealed. It is a game, like Cluedo, only more sophisticated. Most modern-day detective fiction stays true to the rules of the genre: progression of plot and character through to a revealing and satisfying end.

In detective fiction the viewer and reader associate and empathise with the detective, not the murderer. The crime and the violence are usually secondary to the emphasis on motivation, the puzzle, and the detection. The criminal act itself is not of central importance: it is part of the structure, another means of reaching the truth. (Some television detective series like *Spender*, *Taggart* and *The Sweeney* do concentrate on presenting violent realism. Although the central characters have many of the usual personality traits, these programmes come from a different mould in terms of tone and imagery.)

Crime and the whole process of detection have been taking up an increasing amount of broadcast time. Programmes like *Crimewatch UK* compete for viewers along with documentaries, the police soap *The Bill*, and other fictional detective series. In a highly competitive field with new detectives being introduced constantly, the Inspector Morse series has become the most popular, with a success that has been built in spite of the two-hour length, the slow pace, a quiet reflective central character, and the plot's lack of overt violence. (All these qualities are also found in the hugely popular Miss Marple series starring Joan Hickson.) With its base in Oxford presenting a strong sense of our intellectual and cultural heritage (as well as Morse's passion for classical music), and familiar characters who draw the audience into their relationship, it is possible to explain why Morse is so popular. It combines entertainment which is both challenging and secure. We can watch others making order out of chaos, and it all sounds and looks beautiful. But the most enduring images are of Morse himself. For all his arrogance he is a vulnerable figure. Our satisfaction at Morse gaining the truth is offset by our sense of being intrigued by his lonely and unfulfilled private life.

Cast

Morse	John Thaw
Detective Sergeant Lewis	Kevin Whately
Jackie Thorn	Julia Lane
George	Tariq Yunns
Angie Howe	Tess Wajtezak
Jeremy Boynton	Patrick Malahide
Dearden	Richard Huw
Detectives	Al Ashton
	Will Brenton
	Chris Jenkinson
	David Lonsdale
Tim Ablett	Christopher Fulford
Philippa Lau	Carolyn Choa
Whyting Lau	Ken Nazanin
Maitland	Mary Jo Rande
Security Officer	Murray Ewan
Paula Steadman	Cheryl Maiker
Martin Kass	Malcolm Raeburn
Driving Instructor	Kate Doherty
Derek Whittaker	David Ryall
Jimmy	Jake Wood
Sandra	Lynne Morgan
Chief Superintendent Strange	James Grout
Deaf Salesman	Steve Shill
Gerry Firth	Richard Vanstone
Prison Warden	James Duggan

Driven to Distraction

Act One

1   Exterior. Street. Oxford. Early evening.   1

JACKIE THORN is driving home from work. She's a nurse at the Radcliffe. Shopping bags – evidence of a trip to the supermarket – fill the back seat of her Metro. She is stuck in traffic, vehicles at a standstill. She sighs. Her cassette finishes, she ejects it, turns it over, pushes it in.

MORSE is a passenger in the car behind her. LEWIS is driving him to the garage where his beloved Jaguar is being nursed.

> MORSE   What's going on?
>
> LEWIS   Nothing, it's just traffic.
>
> MORSE   *(sly)* No, I think there must be something up ahead . . . Better take a look.
>
> LEWIS   You mean turn on the siren . . . ?
>
> MORSE   Good idea.
>
> LEWIS   *(uncomfortable)* Sir, I can't just, it's anti-social, just to, you always do this.
>
> MORSE   *(grumpy)* The garage will have closed. I won't have my car for the weekend.
>
> *(LEWIS unmoved)*

During this last speech the traffic has moved on a little but in

1

front of them JACKIE hasn't immediately responded. Her cassette has stuck. She tries to eject the cassette. Yards of tape spool out over her hand.

> MORSE Why aren't we moving?

MORSE leans across and presses hard on the horn. LEWIS gives him an aggravated look. MORSE shrugs.

JACKIE jerks forward in the traffic and a shopping bag overbalances. It's one of those days. She turns to give LEWIS a scowl. He mimes an apology.

CREDIT 1

2   Exterior. Oxford. Early evening.   2

JACKIE THORN has managed to battle her way home. She lives in a large building divided into flats. As she pulls up outside it, a second car arrives and slows, parking across the road. We cannot identify car or DRIVER but from his point of view (P.O.V.) we watch JACKIE struggle with her shopping and also the damaged tape. She sets off for the front door, tape streaming behind her. A digital clock glows red on the dashboard. The MAN in the car reaches across to open his glove compartment. He pulls out a roll of wide brown parcel tape. His stereo is playing a torch song. He turns it off. Then gets out of the car.

CREDIT 2

3   Exterior. George's garage. Early evening.   3

The garage is of the lock-up-in-the-alley variety, run by GEORGE, an ex-con who owes MORSE a few favours, one of which is to care for the Jag. He has just locked up as LEWIS turns into the alley. GEORGE makes to get into his own car. MORSE hurries up to him.

GEORGE *(exasperated)* It's too late, Mr Morse, please come back Monday.

MORSE Come on, George . . .

GEORGE *(determined)* Oh please, no.

MORSE *(as LEWIS approaches)* George here is a magician, Sergeant. He can take seven cars and turn them into a single one before your very eyes. Not necessarily his own cars, of course.

CREDIT 3

4 Interior. Jackie Thorn building. Outside Jackie's flat. Early evening. 4

We are on the feet of the unseen DRIVER as he leaves Jackie Thorn's flat. He has some cassette tape wrapped around his feet. We follow this tape up the stairs and along the corridor to Jackie's door. As we arrive the contents of a broken egg swims through the crack at the bottom of the door, the yolk breaking in the process.

CREDIT 4

5 Interior. George's garage. Early evening. 5

MORSE is getting money out of his wallet.

GEORGE *(as MORSE counts out the cash)* Lovely. Mind you, in my opinion, it's good money after bad, 'cause the whole electrics is up the spout for a kick-off.

MORSE What do you mean? This car is pre-electrics. That's why I love it. I don't hold with electrics.

GEORGE Just don't say I never told you.

MORSE opens the door, and pulls off the plastic cover which protects the driver's seat.

> MORSE Oy. This is yours.

CREDIT 5

6   Interior. Jackie Thorn building. Outside Angie's flat. Evening.   6

ANGIE HOWE lives in the flat above Jackie's. She's going out to a party. She comes down the stairs and notices, in the process, the mess outside her neighbour's. It's possible to see that a light is on. She shakes her head and bangs on Jackie's door.

> ANGIE *(vaguely disturbed)* Jackie?
> *(knocking again)* Jackie?

CREDIT 6

7   Interior. Jackie Thorn building. Jackie's flat. Evening.   7

The rest of Jackie's shopping is spilt all over the flat. The CAMERA FINDS her body, shoes and coat abandoned, a chair turned over. We can't see very much, but there's some blood and her hands are bound with brown carpet tape into the prayer position.

Her friend ANGIE has gone downstairs and is using the video entry-phone, whose screen is clearly visible through the door into the hall.

ANGIE's face FADES UP on the screen as the bell is rung and the entry-phone activated.

> ANGIE *(from the screen)* Jackie, let us in, it's me. I'm such a twit, I've left my keys upstairs. Did you know

you've got a bombsite outside your door? Tell
that Tim to get off you – and let me in.
(sing-song) I can see you!
(normal voice) I can't really, but come on, hurry
up!

The entry-phone mouthpiece dangles into space. ANGIE's image
dissolves as the screen blacks out.

CREDIT 7

8 Exterior. Jackie Thorn building. Night.   8

A car arrives at the end of the road, but is waved back by a
police cordon. Blue lights revolve in the black night. A digital
clock glows red on the dashboard. On the stereo we hear the
same torch song. Are we in the murderer's car? It's the same
model, a new Rover. A gloved hand picks up the car telephone
and dials out. The car belongs to JEREMY BOYNTON. He's in his
late thirties, handsome and well-groomed. He owns a garage
and some properties in Oxford. He's thinking quickly.

> BOYNTON *(as the phone is answered by his wife)* Hi. Me. No,
> I'm in the office.
> *(a lie)* I'm just leaving. Want me to pick up an
> Indian?
> *(looks at the flashing lights outside Jackie's
> house)* No, I cancelled . . .
> *(some incredulity on the other end of the phone)* I
> cancelled! Don't believe me, then.

Morse's Jag overtakes him. The cordon tape is lifted up for him
to drive through. BOYNTON puts down his telephone and drives
away from the scene.

9 Exterior. Jackie Thorn building. Night.   9

MORSE arrives outside the house. He is greeted by a young PC,

DEARDEN. MORSE doesn't break stride as he hurries into the house. Someone takes a photograph. A mortuary van is in the BACKGROUND.

> DEARDEN *(as they go inside the house)* It's a repeat of the Maureen Thompson murder, sir. Carbon copy. Brown tape, knife wounds.

10   Interior. Jackie Thorn building. Night.   10

> DEARDEN *(trying very hard)* We've set up an incident room in the downstairs flat, which is empty, sir. I've got Telecom on the way. The victim is upstairs, lives alone, owns her own flat. Same pattern. Do you want to see her first?

MORSE hurries up the stairs.

> MORSE *(muttering)* I can't wait.

> DEARDEN Sir, the boyfriend's up there. Sergeant Lewis is –

But MORSE has disappeared round the landing.

> DEARDEN *(a little miffed)* Speak to yourself.

> MORSE *(suddenly returning)* Get rid of the press – a statement tomorrow – I want a fax machine in the incident room and all of the stuff from the Thompson case, including the polaroids. And get me a coffee. And don't use powdered milk, eh?

11   Interior. Jackie Thorn building. Jackie's flat. Night.   11

MORSE steps gingerly over the broken eggs and tape in the doorway. He registers some of the contents of the shopping bags, a bottle of wine, some Marks and Spencer goodies, a cigar tube. He glances briefly at the BODY, which is partly obscured by other OFFICERS, then addresses ONE of the TEAM. There's a great deal of activity and coming and going and noise. MORSE roots among the shopping, examining the cigar tube – it's a Monte Cristo havana.

> MORSE Where's Lewis?

> OFFICER Kitchen, sir. With the next-door neighbour. She's the one that alerted us.

MORSE heads towards the kitchen.

> MORSE *(over his shoulder)* Any weapon?

> OFFICER Nothing. No prints. Nothing.

> MORSE *(always squeamish)* Clear it all up, will you?

> OFFICER There's a bit of a hitch with the pathologist, that's all.

> MORSE *(stopping and coming back in)* That's all what?

> OFFICER *(a little uneasy)* Well, apparently it's, they've got their AGM or something . . .

> MORSE A pathologists' AGM?

> OFFICER Yeah, apparently, sir.

> MORSE *(the crossword king)* What would you call a group of pathologists?

> OFFICER Sir?

> MORSE *(thinking himself)* You know, like a pride of lions, a murder of ravens, a lamentation of whatever it is.

> OFFICER 2 *(with the video)* Swans.

> MORSE Swans? Swans of pathologists?

> OFFICER 2 Sir, a lamentation of swans.

> MORSE Right.
> *(he's turned and is studying the corpse)* Well, cover

her up, come on. Use a, use something. A body!
A body of pathologists!

During this TIM ABLETT, Jackie's boyfriend, has entered from the
bedroom, the door of which has been ajar. He's holding a
Cookie Monster stuffed toy (from Sesame Street). He's
overwrought. An OFFICER has tried to restrain him from coming
in. This is all very fast.

> OFFICER *(as ABLETT speaks – overlapping)* You can't go in
> there, sir. Please. Sir.

> ABLETT *(of MORSE's remarks)* I think it's obscene. For
> God's sake! For God's sake.

He takes in the full horror of Jackie's murder, loses his balance.

> OFFICER *(over ABLETT's outburst)* It would be much better,
> sir, if we went out and –

LEWIS comes into the doorway behind the OFFICER and ABLETT.

> LEWIS What's going on in here, blooming racket?
> *(sees MORSE)* Oh, hello, sir, sorry I didn't –

> ABLETT *(the scene etching itself on his memory)* You'd
> better find whoever did this before I do, you
> just better find him . . . stand around telling
> each other jokes!
> *(bleak as hell)* She was having my baby. Got any
> jokes about that one?

He starts to cry, uncontrollably. Like a little boy, hugging the
stuffed toy.

And the room goes quiet at this grief.

> MORSE *(moved – and therefore irritable)* Can somebody
> do something, please? Calm him down or take
> him somewhere . . .

> LEWIS *(putting a hand on ABLETT's shoulder)* Come along,
> sir, let's get you sat down somewhere.

The video entry-phone rings and DEARDEN's face appears on the screen.

> DEARDEN *(from the screen)* Can someone tell the Chief I've got Mrs Thorn, the mother, here – and I need to know does he take sugar.

DEARDEN waits expectantly at the screen. SERGEANT LEWIS treads on an egg.

> LEWIS *(grimacing at the mess on his shoe)* Oh, flipping Henry!

> DEARDEN *(on the video screen)* Hello. Is anybody hearing this?

A PATHOLOGIST arrives in a rather flamboyant dinner suit.

12   Interior. Jackie Thorn building. Jackie's flat. Bedroom. Night.   12

The OFFICER is standing over ABLETT who sits on the settee.

MORSE comes in. He nods to the OFFICER to vamoose. He sits down on the settee. It's quiet in here.

> ABLETT *(hoarse)* I've got to go and pick up my kids. I'm late. I have them at the weekend.

> MORSE *(registering this)* Okay. How come you were here?

> ABLETT Angie called me. Jackie's neighbour.

> MORSE But you don't live here?

> ABLETT No, I don't live here.

> MORSE And you were coming for a meal tonight?

> ABLETT No. She was going away for the weekend.

> MORSE The baby, when was it due?

ABLETT *(very distressed)* She found out about three days
ago.

MORSE It wasn't a joke. Not that it makes any
difference. But I, you have to find a way to deal
with these things. That's all. I'm sorry.
(he pulls out the cigar – sniffing it) Smoke?

ABLETT *(blank)* No.

13   Interior. Philippa Lau flat. Night.   13

Darkness. The sound of repeated bell-ringing and knocking. An
oriental woman of about thirty, PHILIPPA LAU, limps along the
hall towards the door without turning on a light. The door is
deadlocked, dog-chained, bolted and has a spyglass. None of
this security is recent. PHILIPPA checks at the spyglass before
unlocking the door.

A Chinese man in his early sixties enters. It's her FATHER.

FATHER *(in Cantonese)* What's happened?

PHILIPPA *(distressed – in Cantonese)* I'm sorry. I'm sorry.
(she's very upset)

FATHER *(calming her)* Calm down, just tell me, tell me.

PHILIPPA On the news, on the news, they said a girl's
been killed, and it all starts up again and I can't
be alone, I can't, I can't . . .
(and the tears come uncontrollably)

Her FATHER comforts her.

14   Interior. Jackie Thorn building. Incident
room. Day.   14

The incident room is in the downstairs flat of the large
detached Victorian house where Jackie and Angie live.

What was intended to be a living-room has been converted into the centre of investigation, with a dozen desks crammed in, telephone lines coiling around them, a fax machine, several computer terminals and wall-boards, some for chalk, some pinboards. Photographs of the victims line another wall. MORSE sits at one end of the room. A DOZEN OFFICERS, including LEWIS and MAITLAND, chairs turned towards him, wait for his briefing. Sergeant Siobhan Maitland, from the Home Office Crime Prevention Course, is in her early thirties – attractive, intelligent, unadorned. What follows is fast, messy, familiar and overlapping. This is a team who work together, where the style has at least the semblance of parity and collaboration. PEOPLE make notes throughout.

MORSE   Okay, what do we know? Apart from Dearden can't remember to buy milk. Similarities, differences . . .

LEWIS   Similarities: single women; young; live alone . . .

OFFICER 1   Car drivers . . .

MORSE   And?

OFFICER 2   Worked in the centre of town.

OFFICER 3   White.

MORSE   Religion?

LEWIS   Nothing.

MORSE   Schools?

OFFICER 4   No, different schools.

MORSE   Doctors? Dentists? Optician?

LEWIS   Nope.

OFFICER 1   What about bank? Building society?

OFFICER 2   No.

DEARDEN   Same letter surname.

11

MORSE Come again?

DEARDEN Thompson. Thorn.

MORSE What would that tell us? Are they both in the phone book? Well someone look. Is this bloke just thumbing through the directory?

OFFICER 2 What about night classes?

LEWIS Clubs? Do we know about clubs?

OFFICER 4 Are they musical? Do they go out dancing?

MORSE What about when they were kids? Were they triangles 1 and 3 in the youth orchestra? Perhaps our man is triangle 2. That's for you, Rendell.

OFFICER 4 writes it down.

DEARDEN *(looking up from the telephone directory – disappointed)* Not in the book.

LEWIS Differences?

OFFICER 3 First murder not sexual.

MORSE *(qualifying this)* Not consummated.

LEWIS Different day of the week. Different location. Maureen Thompson lived in a house, Jackie Thorn lived in a flat.

MORSE *(over this)* Different colouring.

DEARDEN Different cars. Maureen Thompson's car was new . . .

MAITLAND Perhaps you should be looking at this in a different way . . .

MORSE Such as?

MAITLAND Well, we're fairly certain the primary connection between these two women is that they were killed by the same man. Perhaps *he* is what they have in common.

LEWIS I don't follow.

MAITLAND Well, Maureen Thompson worked in the Town Planning Department, Jackie Thorn was a nurse. I don't know – perhaps we should be checking if a man made a planning application and then broke his leg building his conservatory.

She shrugs, smiles, the other OFFICERS respond favourably.

MORSE Why don't you look into that, Sergeant?

MAITLAND Okay.

MORSE Do we all know Sergeant Maitland? She's with us on attachment from Senior CID Training. So if any of you feel like a lecture . . .

LEWIS Sergeant Maitland is an expert on crimes against women.

MORSE Do you have anything to say, Sergeant?

MAITLAND *(walking coolly towards MORSE)* In public? Sure. *(she turns to the rest of the group)* Hello. I'd like to suggest some ways of identifying this man.

She chalks up a stick figure on the board. Adds a question mark. Through what follows she adds speculative remarks as they emerge . . . (i.e. 27 days, Oxford? entry to the house? etc.).

MAITLAND *(cont.)* He's probably self-employed, or not employed, because he can be in place at the end of regular office hours. What does it tell us that there was a gap of 27 days between the two murders? Perhaps he's a sales rep and the murders coincide with his visits to Oxford? But there again, we've had no similar attacks elsewhere. So it would be odd if he didn't live here but only killed here. Though not impossible.

MORSE   I'm not clear if you're saying he knew these women or he didn't.

MAITLAND   Nor am I. He might have just sat in his car and waited for them to pass by, or he might be learning Italian with them at night class. He certainly either knew them or has enough charm to get past their front doors without too much of a commotion.

LEWIS   Perhaps he installs telephones or those video entry things or repairs washing machines or − ?

MAITLAND   *(pointing at the stick man)* Well. Whatever. *(turning to face the men)* But for some reason both these women let this man into their homes and because of it they died.

15   Interior. Bookshop. Day.   15

This is a bookshop near the centre but very uncommercial, small, crowded, full of STUDENTS. Bikes collected in colonies outside. ANGIE is working here.

BOYNTON walks in, looks marvellously out of place. He waits near ANGIE who is advising a would-be CUSTOMER of books on Shiatsu massage. The CUSTOMER takes the recommended volume to the cash desk. ANGIE notices BOYNTON.

BOYNTON   Hello.

ANGIE   *(wary)* Hello Jeremy.

BOYNTON   I was passing. I wanted to say, you know, terrible, terrible, about Jackie.

ANGIE   Yeah.

BOYNTON   You must be devastated. I am.

ANGIE looks uncomfortable. She nods towards the enquiry desk where a queue is building.

ANGIE How did you know I worked here?

BOYNTON Jackie must have mentioned it.

ANGIE Anyway.

BOYNTON What time do you close, Angie?

ANGIE *(defensive)* I've got an evening class.

BOYNTON I just wanted a little chat, a little, just a little chat.

ANGIE As I said, tonight's my evening class.

BOYNTON Let me take you in the car. We can talk on the way.

ANGIE No I don't think so.

BOYNTON I think we should. I think − what's the expression? It's to our mutual benefit. I'll wait. I'll browse. I'm in no hurry. There you are you see.
(he pulls a book at random from the shelf − examines the title) Now, Candida, that's something I've always wanted to know about.

16   Exterior. Supermarket car park. Day.   16

A supermarket car park. Through the windscreen of a parked car, a few shoppers can be seen coming and going.

MAITLAND *(voice-over)* I am the killer. I wait in my car at the end of a working day in a built-up area. I am looking for a young, single woman, driving alone in a smallish vehicle. When I find her I follow her.

In the parked car are MORSE, LEWIS and MAITLAND.

LEWIS Gives you the willies, doesn't it? Some chap is actually doing this.

MORSE How do you know she's single?

MAITLAND You can make a pretty shrewd guess about how somebody lives from how much they buy. You'd know that I lived alone from my shopping basket.

LEWIS *(to MORSE)* That's true of you as well, isn't it? You buy all those dinners for one and stuff.

MORSE grunts. A rather large, plain WOMAN appears with a trolley, including disposable nappies, huge washing powder, etc. and proceeds to unload her purchases into her boot.

MAITLAND So I wouldn't follow her, for instance.

MORSE That's just good taste.

MAITLAND *(combative)* That's just sexist.

MORSE Okay, I wouldn't want to make a connection between sexism and good taste, but fair enough.

MAITLAND Keep on buying the meals for one, sir.

MORSE What's your excuse, Sergeant?

A young WOMAN emerges from the supermarket carrying a couple of bags.

LEWIS Here's one.

MAITLAND Looks promising.

The WOMAN drives off, MAITLAND AND CO. behind her.

MORSE I'm still not sure what this is supposed to achieve.

LEWIS I think we're finding out how easy it is to attack single women.

17   Exterior. Bookshop. Closing time.   17

The shop is closing. ANGIE comes out, is relieved not to find

BOYNTON lurking. She hurries off. A car horn blasts noisily. She jumps. BOYNTON winds down the passenger window.

BOYNTON Hop in.

ANGIE gets in. She's wearing a short skirt, which rides up as she sits. She yanks down her skirt.

BOYNTON *(calculated)* Nice outfit. So, where to?

ANGIE Honestly, it's really not far. I could get a bus.

BOYNTON Don't you need books for the evening class?

ANGIE No.

BOYNTON What's the course?

ANGIE Italian.

BOYNTON E vero? I thought you were going to say gardening.

ANGIE I haven't got a garden.

BOYNTON No, but you like growing plants, don't you?

ANGIE Yeah. What do you mean?

BOYNTON I can never remember the Latin names for these things. You know, pot plants . . . pot plants . . .

ANGIE *(jumpy)* Come on.

BOYNTON I expect you've had to put them under the bed with all those bobbies snooping about.

ANGIE shifts uncomfortably.

BOYNTON *(cont.)* I tell you what's on my mind. I mean obviously I like nothing better than to take a sexy girl for a ride but uh –

ANGIE Give me a break.

BOYNTON Now, see, that's a question I'm always asking myself. Why is it that you ladies wear those

17

tiny skirts which by no stretch of the
imagination — no stretch — you could call prim,
could you, really? And yet when a chap notices
you get all aggravated. That's a mystery to me.

ANGIE I think it's my business what clothes I wear.

BOYNTON 'Course it is. Of course it is. No, get to the
point, Jeremy. It struck me that you and me
have got these little secrets about each other.
Your, uh, smoking habits, my friendship with
poor Jackie.

ANGIE I won't say anything.

BOYNTON Terrific. I'll tell you what. A girl like you
shouldn't have to rely on buses. Why don't you
come and see me sometime and we could fix
you up with a really special deal on a little car?

ANGIE I don't think so.

BOYNTON Well, if you change your mind. Anytime. Tell
you what, I'm a little late. I'm going to drop
you off. Why don't you get yourself a taxi the
rest of the way?

He pulls out a fifty-pound note, lays it on her lap.

ANGIE No thanks.

BOYNTON Suit yourself.

ANGIE gets out.

BOYNTON Ci vidiamo, eh?

His car pulls away.

18   Exterior. Police Records Office. Day.   18

The WOMAN drives past a sign which says 'Thames Valley

Criminal Records Office'. MORSE, LEWIS and MAITLAND pull up behind.

> MORSE Curiouser and curiouser, said Alice.

The WOMAN is stopped at the gate, hands over her ID, exchanges a familiar word or two with the DUTY OFFICER, and drives through the raised barrier.

MAITLAND drives up. The DUTY OFFICER peers in.

> DUTY OFFICER 'Evening, sir.

> MORSE Who was that ahead?

> DUTY OFFICER She's a Computer Officer, sir. Cathy. Night shift.

> MORSE Is she married?

> DUTY OFFICER Oh yes, husband's on the force.

> MORSE *(as if he's proved his point)* Think I'll get out here, Lewis. I'll see you in the morning at the incident room. 'Night, Sergeant Maitland. Thanks for the ride. Will we see you tomorrow?
> *(managing to make this pejorative)* Or are you teaching?

> MAITLAND Yes, I can be there if you want me.

> MORSE Don't ask me, ask Sergeant Lewis. He asked you up here.

> MAITLAND What's his problem?

19 Exterior. Street. Oxford. Early evening.   19

ANGIE is going home. She walks along, the house a little way off. It's still light. A voice from the shadows startles her.

> ABLETT Angie?

She spins, startled, agitated.

> ANGIE Oh God! Oh God.

ABLETT Sorry, I didn't mean to startle you.

ANGIE Oh God, Tim, don't ever do that!

ABLETT (gently) I'm sorry. Of course, I didn't think. I had to catch you before you got to the house, it's crawling with police. Listen, can we go somewhere? I need to talk to you.

20   Interior. Launderette. Early evening.   20

ABLETT has clothes in the wash. His machine stops. He goes over and opens it up.

ANGIE I'm not staying there, Tim. I can't. I'm going to go over to a girlfriend's place. I can't sleep. I'm terrified.

ABLETT (pulling out clothes) The colours have all run. Sod it.

ANGIE (coming over) You shouldn't put whites in with the other stuff.

ABLETT (over this) Oh sod it. I can't even wash my own knickers.
(then, getting to the point) They made me do a blood test. The police. Why do you think that was?

ANGIE I don't know.

ABLETT Do you think I'm a suspect?

ANGIE Well, I expect they'll want to test all the men who knew her.

ABLETT What do you mean, all the men? How many men are there?

ANGIE That's not what I meant. You know what I mean.

ABLETT I don't. I'm asking you. Was she seeing anybody else?

ANGIE I was just her neighbour, Tim.

ABLETT Why did she have all that shopping? She was supposed to be going away for the weekend to see Lorna thing. I rang Lorna and she was really, I could tell she was bluffing. Did you see anybody? Before it happened?

ANGIE No, no, I didn't. Truly.

ABLETT How did this guy get into her flat? If she didn't know him? You know how careful she was . . .

ANGIE *(hadn't really thought of this)* I don't know. I don't know.

21   Exterior. Oxford. 5.30 pm.   21

PAULA STEADMAN and her friend RACHEL FARRADAY come out of the Building Society where they both work. They're young cashiers. They're in the process of buying a flat together. Our perspective of the scene is from a parked car. The girls banter cheerfully but we don't hear what they say. RACHEL wants to go over to the unoccupied flat and measure up. PAULA doesn't. They walk around the corner to Paula's car. PAULA drives away in her car. RACHEL waves.

22   Exterior. Road. Oxford. Early evening.   22

We see PAULA drive off from the interior of a car following her. Torch music plays, the digital clock glows red.

End of Act One

Act Two

23   Morse's car. Lunch time.

MORSE is sitting with a liquid lunch − a bottle of beer −
listening to a very loud burst of Bach. The music is in its final
throes. Perched on the dashboard are some photographs of the
victims, and a set of statements and Jackie Thorn's cheque
book. He is looking through a pile of photos. LEWIS taps on the
window and shocks him from his reverie.

>   LEWIS Sir . . .

MORSE puts up his hand to silence him and they wait in silence
as the music finishes.

>   MORSE What's the problem?

>   LEWIS Nothing, just a social visit.

>   MAITLAND We were just getting some air. Can we join
>   you?

MORSE nods. They get in.

>   MORSE So, any progress?

>   LEWIS No. We can't turn up a thing. I think if they'd
>   even sat on the same bus together we'd know
>   by now. What about you? Anything interesting?

>   MORSE Not really.
>   (he flicks through a cheque book) Sad, isn't it −
>   how all the domestic things become ridiculous
>   when someone dies. She'd just paid her gas bill,
>   her telephone bill, had the car serviced − still
>   had the seat, the plastic sheet over the seat. I
>   had a friend who died, he'd been ill for ages
>   and, and he was worried about − that his car
>   battery would go flat. Every Friday I used to go

round and drive the car around the block for
twenty minutes, keep it . . .
(sighs) . . . and then he died. He hadn't driven
the car in a year.

MAITLAND   That's something I notice these women did have
in common. Both kept their cars really well
looked after. I think there are things growing
and crawling about in mine.

MORSE   They weren't the same make, were they?

LEWIS   No, Maureen Thompson's was new . . .

MORSE   *(interrupting)* Do we know what she drove
before?

LEWIS   I can find out.

MORSE   Go on then.

LEWIS   Right.
(realises he's been dismissed) Oh, right.

MORSE and MAITLAND sit in silence.

MAITLAND   The worst thing is, while we chase our tails,
while we uh, he's out there somewhere and he's
going to do it again.

MORSE   That's right.

MAITLAND   Can we listen to the other side?

MORSE   What? The Bach?

MAITLAND   *(as he shoves in the tape)* I love this music.

MORSE   *(pleased by her enthusiasm)* It's wonderful.

The music begins. Swells.

MORSE   *(cont.)* Listen, I'm sorry if I've been —

MAITLAND, imitating him, puts up a hand for silence.

MAITLAND   Ssshhh.

They listen. Then she smiles. Then so does he.

24 Interior. Jackie Thorn building. Incident room. Lunch time. 24

A fax machine pumps out some information. LEWIS, standing by the machine, grabs it, reads, is very interested in what it says, hurries to the window. He climbs out.

25 Exterior. Jackie Thorn building. Lunch time. 25

MORSE and MAITLAND still in the Jag. LEWIS comes out of the building and goes to the rear of Jackie's car.

> LEWIS *(excited)* Sir! Maureen Thompson traded in a Metro three months ago. She bought it originally from Boynton's Garage, Burford Road.

He bends over the rear window of the Thorn car and reads from the sticker.

> LEWIS *(cont.) (reads)* That's Boynton's Garage.

> MORSE Let's go.

He gives LEWIS his bottle of beer. LEWIS jumps into the Jag. MORSE looks at MAITLAND who puts on her seat belt. The car roars off.

26 Exterior. Boynton's Garage. Afternoon. 26

A sign proclaims: 'BOYNTON'S LTD'. The Morse jag drives up into the forecourt. The TEAM emerge. LEWIS sees something and his memory is jogged.

> LEWIS I knew I knew this place from somewhere. See over there –

LEWIS points to a sign opposite: 'OXFORD DRIVING CENTRE'. MAITLAND hangs back to listen, while MORSE leans on his car looking bored.

LEWIS   That's where Val, Mrs Lewis, my wife, that's
         where she learned to drive. You know, she
         failed her test five times. Just couldn't do it.
         Anyway, three weeks at that place with the top
         man, great bloke – what's his name? It'll come
         back to me – she sailed through. Mind you, that
         was a few years ago now. Drives better than
         me, now.

MORSE   *(impatient)* When you've finished the life and
         times of Sergeant Lewis . . . Do you think we
         can?

LEWIS   Sorry, sir.
         (they head for the showroom) What was his name?
         Tip of my tongue.

27   Interior. Boynton's Garage. Showroom.
         Afternoon.   27

LEWIS and MAITLAND ramble around one part of the showroom,
while MORSE goes elsewhere to investigate a rather beautiful
new Jaguar. He doesn't seem very impressed. He's sitting in it,
when he notices BOYNTON emerge and go over to the Morse
mobile outside. BOYNTON gives the car a swift perusal, opening
the door, checking the mileage, then walks towards the
showroom, catching MORSE's eye.

BOYNTON comes into the showroom. By this time LEWIS and
MAITLAND are talking to a SALESMAN.

BOYNTON sidles up to MORSE.

BOYNTON   You're sitting in pound for pound the best
           luxury convertible on the road.

MORSE   Very nice.

BOYNTON   Beautiful.
           (levelly) That's not a salesman chat-up, by

the way, I can't get enough of them to sell, Mr uh − ?

MORSE Morse.

BOYNTON That your Mark Two outside, Mr Morse?

MORSE Yeah.

BOYNTON Lovely car. That's a real motor car.

MORSE Very real.

BOYNTON No, she's lovely. Needs a little love and attention, if you don't mind me saying so, but lovely. Tell you what, Mr Morse, why don't you hop out, I'll have someone put this on the road, and you take it out for a little spin. I think I could do something very special on a part-x for you. As it happens, I collect old examples of the Jaguar motor car. I've got a D-type, two E-types − one with 9 miles on the clock, genuine, a B-type, which is very rare . . . a −

MORSE (interrupting) Keep going, you'll soon have the whole alphabet.

BOYNTON doesn't like being sent up.

BOYNTON Are you looking seriously, Mr Morse? Or are you whiling away your lunch break?

MORSE holds up his ID badge.

MORSE No, I'm very serious. and it's Chief Inspector Morse, Mr uh − ?

BOYNTON Boynton.

MORSE gets out of the Jag and faces him.

BOYNTON (cont.) I wish you'd said. Makes me look a bit foolish . . .

MORSE Yeah.

BOYNTON *(curt)* So how can I help you?

MORSE Does the name Jackie Thorn mean anything to you?

BOYNTON No. Jackie Thorn? No.

MORSE Maureen Thompson?

BOYNTON No. I have to say it was only seeing your car which drew me out from my office. I don't normally deal directly with customers.

MORSE Right. Right. And yes, well guessed, they were customers of yours.

BOYNTON Has there been a problem, can I ask? Has there been some kind of accident?

MORSE No. You mean with one of your cars? No. No, they're both murder victims, Mr Boynton. They're both dead. And you know — we couldn't find a single thing they had in common. *(smiles)* And then we found you.

28 Interior. Boynton's Garage. Office. Afternoon.   **28**

BOYNTON's back in his office, after the interview with MORSE. KASS comes in.

KASS They're going.

BOYNTON Did they get what they wanted?

KASS I don't think they knew what they wanted. A bit of a wild goose chase in my view.

BOYNTON That's the impression I got.

BOYNTON goes to the window.

KASS I remember the Thorn girl. You must remember her. Very tasty actually. Legs up to her knickers.

I tell you what's creepy: I made a bit of a play
for her, just casual, like you do. Now she's dead.
That's creepy, isn't it?

BOYNTON stays at the window, watching MORSE, LEWIS and
MAITLAND grouped by the Jag.

29   Exterior. Boynton's Garage. Forecourt. Afternoon. 29

MORSE looks back towards the office. Then over towards the
driving centre.

MORSE So you know the chap who runs that place?

LEWIS I used to, well you heard me saying about Val,
but we sent some joy-riders up here as well at
one time, get it out of their systems, let them
drive round a bit. They've got a track and a
skid-pan and so on.

MORSE, who's hardly listening, seems satisfied.

MORSE Why don't we walk round and say hello.

LEWIS *(bewildered)* Now?

MORSE Yes, now.

LEWIS Any particular reason?

MORSE No.

LEWIS We can drive in. There's a big car park.

MORSE No, we'll leave the car here. Let Mr Boynton
have a good look at it.

30   Interior. Boynton's Garage. Office. Afternoon. 30

BOYNTON *(irked — as the GROUP walk away)* Now what?

KASS comes to the window.

>KASS Looks like they're going to the school.

>BOYNTON I think our friend, Chief Inspector Morse, could prove to be something of a major pain in the rectum area.

31   Exterior. Access to the driving centre. Afternoon.   31

The TEAM walk down the long approach to the collection of Nissen huts which constitute the offices and teaching rooms of the driving centre.

>MAITLAND Can I ask what's on your mind, sir?

>MORSE I'd just like my car to sit on Mr Boynton's toes a little longer.

>MAITLAND I get the impression you haven't fallen in love . . .

>MORSE He kept calling it *her, she, the old girl.*

>MAITLAND I hate that. Makes my blood boil.

>MORSE Yes. Everyone knows cars have got nothing to do with women.

He grins. This has become a game between MAITLAND and MORSE. And they're quite enjoying it.

32   Exterior. Driving centre. Skid-pan. Afternoon.   32

A car is being driven fast on a wet surface and goes into a full skid.

33   Interior. Car. Skid-pan. Afternoon.   33

The occupants of the car recover from the skid.

> WHITTAKER   Phew. All right, Jimmy, let's see if you can get
> us back to the office in one piece.

> JIMMY   Okay, Mr Whit.

34   Interior. Driving centre. Room. Afternoon. 34

The screen of what could be an amusement video machine, but
is in fact a driving simulator. A WOMAN is steering her car
around some basic traffic obstacles, sitting at what is essentially
the standard car controls, gears, pedals, steering wheel. An
infinitely patient FEMALE INSTRUCTOR at her shoulder allows
herself a sigh.

> INSTRUCTOR   Check your mirror, indicate. No, remember,
> Gloria, we stop for the junction. Brake, change
> down, brake, get the right foot off the throttle,
> off, off, lovely.

There are half-a-dozen such machines, half-a-dozen such TEAMS
in swing. A mixture of male and female drivers and instructors,
a mixture of racial types and ages. MORSE, LEWIS and MAITLAND
disturb the class.

> INSTRUCTOR   *(cont.)* Yes?

> LEWIS   Sorry. Excuse us. We're looking for Mr uh – the
> chap who's in charge. Sorry.
> *(frowning at MORSE)* It's on the tip of my tongue.

> INSTRUCTOR   Whittaker?

> LEWIS   Whittaker! Derek Whittaker! Thank God for
> that. I would have lain awake all night.

WHITTAKER and JIMMY enter.

> WHITTAKER   Sergeant Lewis, isn't it? Is it?

LEWIS That's right. Mr Whittaker, let me introduce
you, this is Chief Inspector Morse and this is —

He's cut short as WHITTAKER suddenly sinks to his knees, drops
to them clutching his side. LEWIS goes to him, concerned.

LEWIS *(cont.)* Mr —

LEWIS helps him, holds him steady.

WHITTAKER *(blowing — strained)* Ach! It's okay. I'm okay.
That's you, Jimmy.
(to MORSE) I got thrown against the car door
just now. We were a bit ambitious on the
skid-pan.

JIMMY Sorry Mr Whit.

WHITTAKER No, no, I'm fine. I'm fine. I think I gave my ribs
a whack.

MAITLAND Why don't you sit down for a second?

WHITTAKER Thanks, oohh. Don't look so worried. I'll be
right as rain.

35 Interior. Driving centre. Whittaker's office.
Later.   35

JIMMY has brought in a tray of tea and WHITTAKER, behind his
desk and looking a little less pale, takes a sip.

WHITTAKER That's better.
(sips) So, what's the problem? Got some more
tearaways for me to tame — Jimmy was one, do
you remember, Sergeant? On the straight and
narrow now, eh Jimmy?
(JIMMY grins sheepishly) Going to be an instructor
himself soon.
(JIMMY exits — of JIMMY) He's a good lad, they all
are, it's a lifetime in and out of homes, borstals,

remand schools, that's the pig for them, you know.

LEWIS Actually, we're not, although you're right we should bring a few lads up. No, we were up this way and the Chief Inspector was anxious to have a little look round.

WHITTAKER Oh, well it's humble but it's home.

His office, a prefab, is full of DoT posters and 'Don't Drink and Drive' admonishments.

MORSE You get your vehicles from the Boynton Garage?

WHITTAKER Most of them, yes. The heavy vehicles we get elsewhere but yes we have a fleet deal with them. Makes sense, being just next door.

MORSE And they treat you well?

WHITTAKER Oh yes. Of course all these firms like driving-school business, it's a good advertisement, isn't it?
(rhetorical) How many people buy a car the same as the one they learned on?

MORSE Is it Boynton himself you do business with?

WHITTAKER No, to be honest it's mostly Martin Kass, know him? The Sales chappie. Or Ron in servicing. I know Jeremy, of course.

MORSE He seems very nice.

WHITTAKER Yes. He's all right.

Sips his tea.

MORSE Go on.

WHITTAKER What's he done?

MORSE   Nothing. No, no, nothing. He wants to buy my car.

LEWIS   An old Jag.

WHITTAKER   Oh yes, well, he would do.

MORSE   Can I trust him?

WHITTAKER   I wouldn't like to say. Oh, I should think so. Different if it were the young lady . . .

MAITLAND   Oh, why's that?

WHITTAKER   He likes his pretty girls.

MORSE   So we hear.

WHITTAKER   Oh, you've heard? Well, it's common knowledge. Goes together, apparently, love of beautiful cars, love of the ladies. And you say you have a Jaguar yourself?

36   Interior. Boynton's Garage. Office. Day.   36

BOYNTON's in his office. He watches the THREESOME return to the Jag. He's smoking a cigar. MORSE looks up as they reach the car, catches the movement in the venetian blinds which hang in the window of the office. BOYNTON has relaxed, thinking he's got shot of them.

37   Exterior. Boynton's Garage. Forecourt. Day.   37

MORSE   *(to his SERGEANTS – who've got in the car)* Won't be a minute.

MAITLAND   Now what?

LEWIS   Don't ask me.

MAITLAND *(absolutely mystified)* And why are we visiting driving schools?

38   Interior. Boynton's Garage. Office. Day.   38

BOYNTON looks up as his secretary (SANDRA) enters.

SANDRA *(leading in MORSE)* A Chief Inspector Morse.

BOYNTON *(thin smile)* Inspector? Second thoughts about the car?

MORSE No, no, just forgot to ask you something.

BOYNTON *(fantastically pleasant)* What was that now?

MORSE is sniffing the air.

MORSE You are a cigar smoker?

BOYNTON Now and then, yes. Why? Do you want one?

MORSE Mmm. Wouldn't say no.

BOYNTON offers MORSE a Monte Cristo from a large wooden box.

MORSE *(cont.) (appreciative)* Thank you. Thank you very much.

He savours the aroma.

BOYNTON Could be construed as a bribe.

MORSE What for?
(of the cigar) Monte Cristo?

BOYNTON *(rolling his own cigar around his fingers)* A man who drives a Jag and knows his cigars is a man after my own heart, Inspector.

MORSE *(smiles)* I don't smoke actually. I was going to take it back to 11 Dexter Street – that's where Jackie Thorn, who you don't know, that's where Jackie lived – and try to find a speck of ash to match it with. Where were you last Friday evening, by the way?

BOYNTON *(agitated)* Hang on, just hang on a, one thing at a time. What do you mean, match it? I told you I didn't know this woman!

MORSE Then you've got absolutely nothing to worry about.

BOYNTON I spent last Friday evening with my wife and daughter.

MORSE There you are. Better and better.

BOYNTON I have to say I'm getting a little bit aggravated.

MORSE *(remorsefully)* I do that. I rub people up the wrong way.
(holds up the cigar) Thanks again.

39   Exterior. Boynton's Garage. Forecourt. Day. 39

MORSE Well, that's our man all right.

LEWIS *(astonished)* What? Who?

MAITLAND Boynton?

MORSE Now all we need to do is find out how, and why.

Starts car.

MAITLAND What evidence do you have?

MORSE Not a shred.

KASS watches them leave.

40   Exterior. Street. Oxford. Evening.   40

A car drives along the street. It's the old Beetle belonging to

PAULA. She parks. Gets out. We hear the torch music on the track. It comes from a car following her. The headlights obliterate make and driver as the car draws to a halt directly opposite the flat where Paula lives. The lights go off. Lights go on in Paula's flat.

We see her walk into the living-room. Something makes her turn and look out into the street. She draws the curtain. A few beats later headlights re-appear, the engine turns over and the car eases away.

41   Exterior. Street. Oxford. Evening.   41

The Jericho area.

More headlights. The lights go off and a MAN emerges from the car and walks towards his house, a small terraced dwelling.

As the MAN is putting a key into the door, MORSE steps out from the shadows.

>   MORSE Mr Ablett?

ABLETT is startled to find MORSE waiting for him.

42   Interior. Jackie Thorn building. Angie's flat. Evening.   42

ANGIE is watering plants. She goes downstairs and hears repeated knocks on the door.

>   ANGIE Hello.

>   MAITLAND Hello, Angie. It's Sergeant Maitland. Could I come in for a few minutes?

43   Interior. Ablett's house. Kitchen. Evening. 43

ABLETT is making tea in a kitchen sorely in need of some

attention. He has to wash out cups and spoons in order to prepare the drink. It's a tip.

> ABLETT The place is a tip, sorry.

> MORSE Don't worry.

> ABLETT I only seem to be here at weekends and then I have the kids and it's pretty much pandemonium. Jackie refused to set foot in the place.

> MORSE *(asking him not to apologise)* Listen, I'm not —

> ABLETT It's embarrassing. And I've let it go even more. *(he sighs — he's pretty miserable)* What's the point?

He pours out the tea.

> MORSE You're late home tonight.

> ABLETT I work late. It's not a nine-to-five job.

> MORSE No, it's just I called your office and they seemed to think you'd left some time ago.

> ABLETT What are you getting at?

> MORSE Nothing. Just curious.

> ABLETT I went for an Indian. I had a take-away. Chicken tikka masala. Do you want to smell my breath?

> MORSE Jackie's baby — is it possible you weren't the father?

44   Interior. Jackie Thorn building. Angie's flat. Living-room. Evening.   44

MAITLAND and ANGIE are both sitting down.

> MAITLAND What about Tim, her boyfriend?

> ANGIE I like him. He makes me laugh.

MAITLAND Did they have a good relationship?

ANGIE Yes, I think so. Yes. I really didn't know them that well.

MAITLAND *(easily)* Oh, I thought you'd been on holiday with Jackie?

ANGIE I think they had a pretty good relationship, yes. *(irritable)* Look, I'm too tired to do this now. If you want to interrogate me, can it wait until the morning?

MAITLAND *(nicely)* Okay, I'll go. It wasn't my intention to interrogate you. One thing, there wasn't any other visitor to Jackie's flat, was there?

ANGIE There's bound to have been. She was a really popular girl. She had a lot of friends.

MAITLAND I meant other men . . .

ANGIE As I said, she had lots of friends.

MAITLAND But clearly Tim Ablett was her boyfriend.

ANGIE Yeah.

MAITLAND gets up and goes towards the door.

MAITLAND Does the name Jeremy Boynton mean anything to you?

ANGIE Jeremy what?

MAITLAND Boynton.

ANGIE No. Why? Is he supposed to be one of Jackie's friends?

MAITLAND His name cropped up.

The telephone rings.

MAITLAND *(cont.)* Don't mind me.

ANGIE No, it's all right. I'll leave it.

MAITLAND No, really, I'll go. Perhaps another time will be more . . . I can let myself out.

ANGIE Okay.

She stands, they both do. The phone rings.

ANGIE *(cont.)* Okay.

MAITLAND *(nicely)* I'll see you.

ANGIE waits until she hears the door open and shut, then grabs the phone.

ANGIE *(into the phone — a little cautious)* Hello?
(her face falls — worst fears realised) Yes.
(listens) Yes.
(listens) No, I didn't.
(clearly interrupting) I didn't.
(listens) Stop hassling me, would you.
(listens) If you must know, they've just been here.
(listens) Yes.
(listens) Nothing, your name came up and I didn't say anything.
(listens) They, she just said did I know you, you'd been a friend of Jackie's.
(listens) I told you, I didn't tell them a thing.
(listens — she's being threatened — she's frightened) Okay. Okay. Okay.

The phone has gone dead. She puts down the receiver, and puts her hands over her face.

45 Interior. Jackie Thorn building. Incident centre. Morse's office. Morning. 45

MORSE works in his own room of the flat co-opted for the incident centre. It's a bedroom and there are still vestiges of a pretty room, and a mattress overwhelmed with documents and files. It's a little incongruous and very makeshift, with telephone cables trailing, and random bits of furniture.

MAITLAND, LEWIS and MORSE are in pow-wow outside on the patio.

LEWIS   You can't arrest the man just because you don't like him.

MORSE   More's the pity.

MAITLAND   I'm convinced Angie Howe knows something.

MORSE   When will we get confirmation of the lab reports on the DNA tests?

LEWIS   Today or tomorrow.

MORSE   I went to see the boyfriend last night, tried out our little theory.

LEWIS   What do you mean? What theory?

MORSE   That the murderer was also the father of Jackie's child. Same blood type.

LEWIS   But we don't know that!
(outraged) That's not on, sir, that's terrible.

MORSE   What?

MAITLAND   Are you saying you told Tim he might not be the father?

MORSE   I'm saying I put to him he might be the murderer.

LEWIS   *(angry)* As if the lad didn't have enough to grieve about.

MORSE   I'm looking for a motive that will nail Boynton. If he was the father of Angie's child, it would give me one.

MAITLAND   But we haven't even established they knew each other!

40

MORSE   There's a man out there killing young women. He's completely unscrupulous. I want to catch him.

LEWIS   I'm sorry, but I don't think that's the way to go about it. Sir.

MORSE   Boynton was divorced by his first wife. According to the solicitor he was beating her about.

LEWIS   So?

MORSE   So.

MAITLAND   If every man who hit his wife was accused of murder, the courts would be overflowing.

MORSE   Was there anything else, Sergeants?

LEWIS   No.

With a deal of disgruntlement, LEWIS and MAITLAND leave the room. MORSE ponders on the cigar, rolling it in his fingers.

46   Interior. Jackie Thorn building. Incident centre. Hall. Morning.   46

LEWIS and MAITLAND walk back to the incident room in silence. As they reach the door, MAITLAND can contain her feelings no longer.

MAITLAND   Who does that guy think he is?

This annoys LEWIS even more. He wants to defend MORSE, but can't. He pushes past MAITLAND and –

47   Interior. Jackie Thorn building. Incident room. Morning.   47

– walks straight to his desk.

He's hardly sat down when there's a knock at the door. No-one gets up.

> LEWIS *(irritably)* Dearden, come on, get the door will you?

> DEARDEN *(thrown by LEWIS's tone)* Sir.

He walks to the door. ANGIE HOWE is standing with a couple of plants in her arms. She's been crying.

> MAITLAND *(getting up)* Angie? Angie, what's the matter?

ANGIE walks over to her desk and puts the plants down in front of her.

> ANGIE I've got to talk to you.

> MAITLAND What are these?

> ANGIE They're marijuana plants. There are a dozen more upstairs in my tower.

End of Act Two

Act Three

48   Interior. Jackie Thorn building. Incident centre. Morse's office. Day.   48

MORSE is sitting on his makeshift desk in his makeshift office. LEWIS knocks and brings in BOYNTON, MAITLAND behind him. All three police officers, MORSE included, are softly spoken and disconcertingly gentle during what follows.

MORSE Find your way here all right, Mr Boynton?

BOYNTON Yes, thank you.

MORSE Good. You've met Sergeant Maitland?

BOYNTON Yes. That's right. Hello.

MAITLAND Hello.

MORSE And which letter did you pop over in?

BOYNTON Come again?

MORSE The B, C, D or E-type?

BOYNTON *(not amused)* Ha, no, I drive a company car mostly. Just a saloon.

MORSE Good, so you wouldn't be too concerned, if one of my lads takes a look at it? Pulled out the seats and so on.

BOYNTON What do you mean? What's going on?

MORSE Have we offered you tea?

BOYNTON No thank you.
(returning to MORSE's inquiry) Why do you want to look at my car?

LEWIS No need to be alarmed, sir. Just a routine check.

43

MORSE   Make sure you've paid your road tax. Do you
             carry a knife?

BOYNTON   No! What do you mean, a knife?

MORSE   Well, lots of people do. Boy-scout types. In case
             you break down in the middle of the moors or,
             you know, be prepared.

BOYNTON   This is ridiculous! I don't have a knife. Is this,
             can I get this straight, am I being accused of
             something?

MORSE   Not at the moment.

BOYNTON   Because I want my lawyer here.

MORSE   Sure. Can I just confirm, for my memory's sake,
             you're quite certain you hadn't met Jackie
             Thorn?

BOYNTON   I've already told you.

MORSE   No, just making sure I understood you correctly.
             (to MAITLAND) Sergeant, tell us about Angela
             Howe.

MAITLAND   Jackie's neighbour, Angie Howe, seems to think
             you were a friend of Jackie's. Is she making a
             mistake?

LEWIS   She also told us you've made a number of
             threats against her to prevent her from giving
             us this information.

BOYNTON   *(unsettled)* I want my lawyer. I'm not saying
             anything else until my lawyer is here.

MORSE   *(pushing over a telephone – very chummy
             manner)* Go ahead. You should tell him we're
             bringing charges against you. And tell him
             we're intending to do blood tests, fingerprint
             tests, DNA tests, every test we can think of. In
             fact, tell him to bring a few partners with him:

you're going to need all the help you can get, Mr Boynton.

49   Exterior. Jackie Thorn building. Day.   49

DEARDEN leads a sombre-faced BOYNTON into a police car. A SECOND OFFICER is driving. MORSE comes to the entrance, watches the MEN go to work on the Boynton vehicle.

50   Interior. Jackie Thorn building. Incident centre. Morse's office. Day.   50

MORSE returns, and shuts the door.

51   Exterior. Jackie Thorn building/Boynton's car. Day.   51

As MORSE cheerfully predicted, his DETECTIVES quite literally begin to pull the car apart.

An OFFICER in the front passenger seat pulls open the glove compartment, alongside which the dashboard clock glows a pale red in the sunshine. There's nothing there other than receipts and a folded cap and a torch. A cassette is in the stereo − the OFFICER examines it, then replaces it in the machine and turns it on. It's the same music we heard earlier. The back seats start coming out. And the guts of the car accumulate on the gravel.

52   Interior. Jackie Thorn building. Incident room. Afternoon.   52

EVERYONE is on the telephone working hard to find some dirt on Boynton. His name is repeated over and over, desk to desk. What follows is happening simultaneously until STRANGE's entrance.

LEWIS   *(into phone)* Does the name Jeremy Boynton
         mean anything to you, Mrs Thompson?
         Boynton. B O Y N T O N.
         (listens) N. N for Noddy. No, he's older. He
         owns a garage and Maureen bought a car from
         there, no, no, the one before, that's right.
         Boynton.

OFFICER *(into phone)* Boynton.
         Batman-One-Year-Norman-Tommy-One-
         Norman, male, 42, Caucasian.

OFFICER *(into phone)* I've got a case number. Yeah, just
         send the whole lot round in a car.

MAITLAND *(into phone)* That's right: Maureen bought her
         car from him, he has a garage on the Burley
         Road.
         (listens) Okay. Well, can you ask around the
         office for me – it would be really useful?
         (listens) Maitland. Sergeant Maitland.
         *(her caller is checking the telephone
         number)* Exactly. That's wonderful. Thanks.
         Great. 'Bye.

CHIEF SUPERINTENDENT STRANGE walks in during this. His presence
registers in the room.

STRANGE *(to LEWIS)* Where is he?

LEWIS   Just a minute, Mrs Thompson.
         (clasping his hand over the mouthpiece) Sir. He's
         next door, just on your left there.

STRANGE walks straight out. He looks thunderous. And it
registers with the TEAM, who exchange glances and frowns. ONE
of the OFFICERS makes a gesture of slitting his throat.

STRANGE walks straight in to find MORSE lying on the bed, files
and documents scattered to the floor. MORSE has dozed off.

STRANGE   Come on, Morse, for heaven's sake.

MORSE   *(a little abashed at being discovered in the supine
        position)* I was thinking.
        (acknowledging) Sir.

STRANGE   *(raging)* Well listen, I'll go, because clearly
          thinking is at a premium with you.

MORSE   What does that mean?

STRANGE   What do you think you're playing at, mate? I've
          got half the briefs in London on my back, I've
          got the Crown Prosecution Service screaming
          down the phone, I've got —
          (sighing) Oh you know, and you're in bed. It's
          brilliant.

MORSE   Okay, okay, so what have I done now?

STRANGE   I'm going to get Lewis in here and have this
          room ransacked and if I find so much as the
          whiff of a bottle, you're for the high jump.

MORSE looks stung.

STRANGE   *(cont.)* Do you realise you've brought a man
          into custody without a shred of evidence?

MORSE   *(trying to thaw STRANGE)* I've got lots of shreds,
        just not much in the way of substance.

STRANGE   I'm not laughing this off, Morse. You're going
          at this case like a bloody bulldozer.

MORSE   *(serious himself)* I don't think so. I think I've
        found the killer, and no I don't have enough on
        him yet, but we're all working on that, and I'd

rather have him jumping up and down in a cell than putting a knife in another woman while we plod around politely. And I resent your remarks about alcohol. I'm fed up with laughing that off.

STRANGE *(ignoring this)* What basis are you holding him on? The CPS have told me you haven't got the semblance of a case.

MORSE This is a man who can lie brazenly, who can threaten a woman without any compunction, whose first wife left him after he'd beaten her up, who has all the opportunity in the world to carry out these crimes, who certainly was having a relationship with the second victim.

STRANGE How do you know that?

MORSE I just do. I mean, there was a cigar in her shopping, he smokes cigars, she was obviously intending to cook for him the night she died, she was pregnant, I'm sure we're going to find out he was the father. He's married, she puts pressure on him, he loses his temper . . . it's there, it's just, it's there, I know the cigar is a bit weak, but it's a direct connection, and they both had bought their cars through him and −
(shrugs) − and it'll fall into place.

STRANGE And what? He killed the other woman a month earlier in a fit of retrospective rage.

MORSE There'll be a reason. Come on, we've both been at this for too long, you get an instinct, you know, I know this man did it. He covers his tracks, that's the style, and it's all about bluff. So now I'm bluffing him. Tomorrow I'll get the results of the blood tests and then we turn the screw until he owns up.

STRANGE No. You let him go. If you don't, I will. You

put together a case . . . a watertight case, and
then you charge him. No, then you come and
see me. I want him out of custody, now. Don't
go back to bed.

And he's gone.

54   Exterior. Jackie Thorn building. Afternoon. 54

STRANGE emerges from the building.

He approaches and surprises an OFFICER standing idly by the
Boynton car. The OFFICER stiffens guiltily to attention.

> STRANGE Get this bloody car back together. And make
> sure every crumb, every hair, every speck of
> dust is back where you found it.
>
> LEWIS You heard the man.
>
> OFFICER What a waste of time.

MORSE comes out and watches STRANGE driving off. He walks
over to the Boynton car and sits on one of the displaced seats.
LEWIS walks round to him.

> LEWIS Sorry, sir: there's sod all. The thing is, this is a
> demo vehicle. It probably gets scrubbed down
> once a day. It's a perfect car to commit crime in.
>
> MORSE Yeah.
> *(staring glumly)* And I know he did it.

The OFFICER needs Morse's seat.

> OFFICER Excuse me please, sir . . .

55   Interior. Thames Valley HQ. Interview
room. Day.   55

BOYNTON is sitting at a bare table while his valuables are

restored to him by the DUTY SERGEANT. He's full of
self-righteous indignation. MORSE arrives.

> BOYNTON *(fastening his belt)* I haven't worked out how I
> can make the most noise about this. But I will.

> MORSE You know, I'd sleep on it if I were you. We'll
> get some results tomorrow and too much sound
> and fury might embarrass you.

> BOYNTON My solicitor has already told me they'd laugh
> you out of court.

> MORSE Maybe.
> *(to the DUTY SERGEANT)* Thank you, Sergeant.

The DUTY SERGEANT leaves the room. The gloves come off in
the exchange.

> MORSE *(cont.)* I think you should think of this as a few
> days off, a sort of holiday. Because you'll be
> back. So don't fly off to Torremolinos for the
> weekend, will you?

> BOYNTON You've got a real attitude problem, you know
> that? It's what gives the police a bad name.

> MORSE That's odd, because since I met you I've
> completely revised my opinion about car
> dealers. Nice chaps, clearly. They threaten
> young women, cheat on their wives, but
> otherwise, you know, terrific guys.

> BOYNTON *(if looks could kill)* Right.

> MORSE Before you go, tell me: if you didn't kill Jackie,
> why did you lie about knowing her?

> BOYNTON Are you married?

> MORSE No.

> BOYNTON *(nods)* Well think about it for a moment.
> *(he reaches the door – turns)* Just try and find the

place where your brain lives. And then stick this
up it.

He shows MORSE his middle finger in a time-honoured gesture.

56   Interior. Philippa Lau flat. Day.   56

PHILIPPA LAU is walking up the stairs to her flat. She carries a
small bag of groceries. She limps along towards her door. Even
in the daytime it's a shadowy corridor.

> MAN   Hello.

A thickset MAN is coming down the corridor. He carries a
suitcase. His voice has the muffled quality of a deaf person. He
is slightly backward. PHILIPPA is terrified out of her mind. The
MAN stands between her and the door to her flat.

> PHILIPPA   *(whimpering)* Please. Oh God. Please don't.

PHILIPPA sinks to the ground, petrified. The MAN approaches
holding up a flimsy plastic card with a photograph attached.

> MAN   *(his voice disturbingly thick and distorted)* Would
> you read my card?

PHILIPPA stares blankly at the MAN. She's weeping. He opens the
suitcase. It's full of domestic cleaners and cloths and sponges
and ironing-board covers.

> MAN   *(cont.)* Please read my card. It tells you who I
> am. I'm learning to sell things. Can I show them
> to you?

> PHILIPPA   *(emerging from the sea of tears)* What?

> MAN   Handkerchiefs. These are very pretty. Can I
> show you? I have all kinds of dusters and
> telephone cleaners and ironing-board covers.

He pulls a pack of handkerchiefs from his case.

> MAN   *(cont.)* Uh, the handkerchiefs are two pounds for
> a set of six.

51

The learner's course seen from the office window. By the
window WHITTAKER is on the phone. He looks pensive.

> WHITTAKER No problem. Mr Morse, I'd be delighted.

58   Interior. Jackie Thorn building. Incident   58
room. Afternoon.

LEWIS comes into Morse's room. MORSE is still speaking to
WHITTAKER.

> MORSE *(into phone)* Okay, good, I'll see you tomorrow.
> Sergeant Lewis has just walked in. I'll ask him to
> lend me his Highway Code.
> *(WHITTAKER asks for his regards to be passed on)* I
> will.
> *(see you tomorrow)* Yeah. 'Bye now.

> LEWIS Who was that?

> MORSE Your friend, Mr Whittaker. I'm going to have
> some driving lessons.

> LEWIS *(perplexed)* Why?

> MORSE You should be pleased. You're always criticising
> my driving.

LEWIS passes him a file.

59   Exterior. Street of Thorn building.   59
Afternoon.

ABLETT and ANGIE stand outside with PETER MAX in a buggy.
MATTHEW stands next to them. They are near the house.

> ABLETT Say goodbye, Matt.

> MATTHEW *(the eldest)* 'Bye.

ABLETT Good boy.

ANGIE 'Bye Matthew.
(*shaking his hand*) And bye-bye Peter Max.

She shakes PETER MAX's hand in the buggy.

A car has pulled out of the drive during these valedictions. It seems to be passing them but then suddenly stops. It's driven by MAITLAND. She winds down the window.

MAITLAND Angie —

ANGIE sees her.

ANGIE Oh, hi.

She walks over to the car. ABLETT hangs back.

MAITLAND (*calling over to ABLETT*) Hello Mr Ablett.

ABLETT nods.

ANGIE Everything all right?

MAITLAND Not too bad. But I think I should tell you, Angie: Jeremy Boynton's been released.

ANGIE What?

MAITLAND There's no evidence to link him with Jackie's murder.

ANGIE (*frightened*) But there must be!

MAITLAND Listen, don't be anxious. If you get any intimidation — you won't, I'm certain — but if he were to try something stupid, we're downstairs. For the time being we'll have an officer in the building twenty-four hours a day.

ANGIE (*turning — bleakly — to ABLETT*) They've let him go.

MAITLAND Angie — it's not a question of letting him go,

it's a question of not having any reason to detain him.

ABLETT has walked up during this exchange. He overhears this last remark.

> ABLETT You mean until he does it again? What about these tests? What about these threats he made to Angie?

> MAITLAND We have to work within the rule of law.

> ABLETT But who does that protect? You know. 'Cause that's the question here, isn't it? Come on, son, come back with me –

> MAITLAND Angie, I promise nothing will happen to you. You have my word on that.

But ANGIE's back with ABLETT and walking away.

> MAITLAND *(cont.)* You've got my word on that. Angie!

> ABLETT Come on, Angie. You can't stay in that flat.

A car behind toots impatiently. MAITLAND drives away.

60   Exterior. Street. Oxford. Early evening.   60

An estate agent's sign: 'Sale Arranged'. From the POINT OF VIEW of a car window we see PAULA and her friend RACHEL standing precariously on the ledges of the bay window of their new flat, measuring up for curtains. The scene is accompanied by the ubiquitous torch song smooching out of the car stereo.

61   Exterior. Street. Oxford. Early evening.   61

A little later and PAULA and RACHEL emerge and get into the Beetle, roaring off. Back to the POINT OF VIEW of the observer's car, which pulls out and follows, the red figures on the digital clock beginning to glow in the failing light.

62   Exterior. Street. Oxford. Evening.   62

As PAULA, now alone, parks and walks to her door, the car
following her slows, parks. The DRIVER of the other car reaches
inside his glove compartment, opens it to reveal the roll of
brown tape, the knife. Closes the compartment. The car door is
opened.

The MAN – we can't identify him – gets out, closes the door.
As he walks towards the house, PAULA's life is involuntarily and
temporarily saved. Just as she is walking towards her door she
sees an ELDERLY NEIGHBOUR struggling with a ludicrous number
of black plastic rubbish bags. She's very friendly with PAULA,
who grabs one of the bags and goes with her to where the
dustbins are kept. The WOULD-BE ASSAILANT, thwarted, turns and
goes to his car.

63   Exterior. Boynton's Garage. Burford Road.
Morning.   63

BOYNTON drives into the forecourt, cigar smoke drifting out in
plumes. The smile of a man freed from antagonism disappears
when he sees the Morse Jag parked over at the far end of the
forecourt.

64   Exterior. Open road. Morning.   64

MORSE is driving.

> WHITTAKER   We'll take the second exit, please.

MORSE obeys. WHITTAKER observes closely, writes something on
his clipboard.

> MORSE   You're making me nervous.

> WHITTAKER   What's the speed limit on this road?

> MORSE   *(doesn't know)* Uh, thirty.

WHITTAKER nods towards a sign on a lamppost. It says 40.

    MORSE *(cont.)* Forty.

WHITTAKER puts a card over the rear-view mirror.

    WHITTAKER What's behind you?

    MORSE Erm, well, I don't think there was – er –

WHITTAKER removes his hand. There is a vehicle behind them.

    WHITTAKER What speed are you doing?

MORSE brakes.

    MORSE Too fast, I'm going a bit fast, I suppose.

65   Exterior. Boynton's Garage. Day.   65

ABLETT is standing on the forecourt. He is looking at the glass window of Boynton's office. A tanker draws up, and parks, obscuring his vision. ABLETT walks over to the showroom and takes notice of the proceedings with the petrol tanker.

66   Exterior. Open road. Day.   66

MORSE is driving again. He's having to explain what he's doing and seeing on the road as comprehensively as he can. We hear this appropriate commentary interspersed with WHITTAKER's instructions which, depending on the conditions and situation, go something like this.

    WHITTAKER *(over MORSE's own commentary)* Brake, no – off
               the brake, off . . . you're braking too hard too
               late, feather, feather the brake, wrong gear . . .
               don't miss out the second and third gears,
               they're there for a reason, speed! Watch the
               revs, position, position.
               (relaxes a little) How are we doing?

MORSE shakes his head, puffs out, exhausted.

WHITTAKER *(cont.) (amused)* Let's head back. I think that's enough for the first go.

MORSE *(rueful)* Should I put L-plates on?

WHITTAKER You're not so bad. We'll make a driver out of you yet.

MORSE drives.

WHITTAKER *(cont.)* I can't help wondering — what made you get in touch?

MORSE Jeremy Boynton gave me the idea.

WHITTAKER Jeremy?

MORSE I think he liked the idea of my being able to pop in on a regular basis.

67 Interior. Boynton's Garage. Office. Morning. 67

BOYNTON's on the phone to his solicitor.

BOYNTON *(into phone — still raging)* — I'm not being hysterical, it's aggravation. Hang on, wait a minute. What am I paying you for? If you don't agree with me, get me somebody on the phone who does. The guy's a little bully-boy. That's not a personal theory: it is a fact.

During this, SANDRA has come in, is hovering, a little anxiously.

BOYNTON *(cont.)* What?

SANDRA Someone to see you, sir. Says it's urgent.

BOYNTON I'm paying a fortune for this call, have you seen what these guys charge me for a bloody telephone call, so don't, use some initiative, will you?
(back into phone) What was I saying?

SANDRA   I know, Mr B, but this man says he can't wait.

And with that ABLETT walks casually into the room.

BOYNTON   Look, Julian, I'm going to have to call you back. *(to ABLETT)* What do you want?

ABLETT   Good morning, Mr Boynton.

BOYNTON   What do you think you're doing just walking straight into my office?

ABLETT   My name's Tim Ablett, Mr Boynton.

BOYNTON   *(not clicking at first)* I don't care what your name —
(then dawning) Ah, hang on, right.

ABLETT   *Ah, hang on, right.*

BOYNTON   *(cornered)* Well, what, what do you want? Now's not exactly a very good time if —

ABLETT   *(to SANDRA)* I'd take a little walk, if I were you.

SANDRA   What?

ABLETT   *(a little crazed)* Get out of here.

He starts pacing the office.

BOYNTON   Yes, go on, Sandra, go and paint your nails, or something.

ABLETT   You've got a real way with the ladies, eh Jeremy? Real style.

BOYNTON   Listen, okay, let's try and have a civilised conversation.

ABLETT   So — how come you managed to smarm your way out of police custody? You bastard.

BOYNTON   Because I haven't done anything wrong.

ABLETT   You're a liar and now you're going to get what's coming to you, Mr Boynton.

He turns on his heels and walks out.

BOYNTON picks up the telephone receiver.

> BOYNTON *(apprehensive)* Martin . . .

68 Exterior. Boynton's Garage. Forecourt. Morning. 68

ABLETT emerges from the office, goes straight to the tanker and unscrews the tap, pulling out the hose which begins to spout petrol everywhere, including over ABLETT. He gets it under control just as BOYNTON appears and turns the hose on him. As the TANKER DRIVER, idly sipping at a plastic cup, notices, he drops the cup and charges towards ABLETT, who is by now advancing on BOYNTON, deluging him with petrol. PEOPLE dive for cover at the prospect of an almighty explosion. All hell is let loose.

BOYNTON falls almost unconscious to the ground. ABLETT straddles him and searches his pockets.

> ABLETT Now let's light one of your cigars!

> SANDRA *(in the office on the phone)* Yes, yes, all three.

ABLETT is now hysterical and distressed.

69 Exterior. Whittaker's car. Morning. 69

MORSE is driving back along the Burford Road.

> MORSE So do you see much of Jeremy?

> WHITTAKER We have dealings. Not socially. We used to, a bit. Then he did something, put me in it with his wife.

> MORSE *(interested)* Oh? What was that?

> WHITTAKER Nothing. Doesn't matter.

MORSE *(prompting)* When you say put you in it, you
mean —

WHITTAKER Well let's just say one evening he was with one
party and said he was with me. I don't like —

The sound of an approaching ambulance cuts him short. It
hurtles past them down the road.

70   Exterior. Boynton's Garage. Forecourt. Morning.   70

MORSE swerves into the forecourt, which is now milling with
PEOPLE evacuating the garage. The fire brigade are spraying the
area with foam. It's chaos.

ABLETT is being helped into a police car by a COUPLE OF POLICE
OFFICERS. He has a blanket round him and is wet through. MORSE
walks through the mess.

Then, from the service area, a petrol-drenched BOYNTON, clearly
in a state of shock, on a stretcher, is being lifted into the
ambulance.

MORSE approaches and walks alongside the stretcher.

End of Act Three

Act Four

71 Exterior. Boynton's Garage. Early evening. 71

The drama over at the garage, what remains is a kind of mess, with the detritus of the effort to neutralise the petrol spillage. The scene has a dishevelled look, as if under siege, with the entrances barricaded. There is a scattering of POLICE and MAINTENANCE PEOPLE putting the place back into order. LEWIS, MAITLAND and DEARDEN get out of a car.

72 Interior. Boynton's Garage. Office. Early evening. 72

MORSE is installed in Boynton's office. Piles of files spill over from the desk to the floor. The THREE OFFICERS enter.

MORSE What kept you?

LEWIS Well, sir, you said we were in for a long evening, so I thought we should all get home and eat and . . . I brought you some sandwiches.

MORSE What kind?

LEWIS *(didn't make them – doesn't know)* Oh, well Val made them, uh, salmon, I expect, or cheese and pickle.
(he produces a packet and sniffs it) Yeah.

He hands it over to MORSE, who is flicking through a file. Then he realises that MORSE has been going through Boynton's belongings.

LEWIS *(taken aback)* Is this you, sir?

MORSE Is this me going through Mr Boynton's personal belongings? Absolutely.

LEWIS Do we have a warrant?

MORSE   *(waving the question away)* Not as such.
         (then briskly) So, I'm in here, I want the rest of
         you to go and ransack the business files, the
         customer correspondence, service files. Anything.
         We've got one night to come up with
         something. Then we put it all back in the
         morning.

LEWIS   *(firmly)* No.

MORSE   No, what?

LEWIS   No, we can't do that, sir. It's not legal.

MAITLAND What do you hope to find, anyway?

MORSE   Something, anything, that proves Mr Boynton is
         a killer. It's an opportunity. If we can't find it,
         nobody's hurt, nobody knows. If we come up
         with something, then we come up with
         something . . .

MAITLAND I'm up for it.

MORSE   Good.

DEARDEN Me too.

MAITLAND *(reasonably)* Come on, Sergeant, going through
         car service files is not like reading someone's
         diary.

LEWIS   We should have requested a warrant.

MORSE   I'm not going to get a warrant, am I? So there
         was no point asking. Look, you go home, Lewis,
         if your conscience is pricking you so much.

LEWIS   Yeah. I think I'm going to.

MAITLAND *(mediating like crazy)* Let's just do it.

LEWIS   *(to MAITLAND – feeling compromised on all sides)* I
         thought you stood for – all that stuff about
         working with the community, about community

partnership — what does that mean if you'll go through someone's belongings without asking them or telling them?

MAITLAND Yesterday Tim Ablett and Angie Howe asked me who the law protects, the Boyntons of this world or the Jackie Thorns? And I couldn't answer.

LEWIS I'll see you tomorrow.

LEWIS turns and leaves. DEARDEN is now feeling decidedly uncomfortable.

DEARDEN Actually, sir, uh, I think — uh, it strikes me Sergeant Lewis, he's got a point, actually. Hasn't he?

MORSE Listen, you go, that's fine. That's absolutely fine. Goodnight.

DEARDEN You sure?

MORSE Positive.

DEARDEN (getting up — sidling off) Right, well, I'll see if I can catch — because I haven't got transport — so, anyway, thanks, sir. Goodnight, Sergeant Maitland.

MAITLAND 'Night, Dearden.

And he's gone. MORSE looks at MAITLAND.

MORSE Don't feel obliged.

MAITLAND I don't.

73 Interior. Jackie Thorn building. Incident room. Late night.   73

MORSE and MAITLAND have settled down like a couple of revising students. They're on the floor of the incident room surrounded by boxes (marked with garage produce signs, for engine oil, distilled water, etc.). There are also a couple of empty bottles of beer and a couple of open ones and a pizza box. MAITLAND chews on a slice while she fingers a Roladex, flipping through the names.

MAITLAND Anything?

MORSE No. You know, I think we could get him on tax or something, his car collection is funded very creatively, but I haven't come across anything interesting . . .
(grins) . . . like a knife or − or a love letter from Maureen Thompson . . .

MAITLAND Me neither. My head's spinning. He didn't even give Jackie Thorn a discount on her service. There's nothing here.

They're very close together, it's late, it's strangely intimate.

MORSE Have you had enough?

MAITLAND Nearly. What time is it?

MORSE Late.

MAITLAND Are you always this obsessional?

MORSE You mean the case? I don't know. I don't think so. I don't know. Maybe it's like the Church. My mother always used to say priests should be married, what did they understand if they weren't married? Maybe the same is true of policemen.

MAITLAND Do you not have someone waiting at home?

MORSE No. Do you?

MAITLAND (light − avoiding it) Here? In my digs? Only an old teddy bear.

MORSE And at home-home?

MAITLAND I think so. Yeah.

MORSE *(wistfully)* Well.
(then decisive) Let's pack up. I can take this back.

MAITLAND Right.

They start piling stuff into the boxes. They're quiet, both
wrapped up in their thoughts.

MAITLAND *(cont.) (groping for something)* Tell me again what
we've been looking for.

MORSE I don't know. Something that ties Boynton in
with these murders.

MAITLAND Right, so the only names we've looked for have
been Jackie's or Maureen Thompson's.

MORSE So?

MAITLAND Well, this doesn't make any sense, but why
aren't we looking for some other connection?

MORSE Such as?

MAITLAND Well, what if he's committed similar crimes in
the past . . . that there have been other women
who've come through the garage . . . ?

MORSE I think we'd know.

MAITLAND Why?

MORSE Well, I know the murder cases on our books. I
could recite them.

MAITLAND And they're all closed?

MORSE Not all of them . . . but none which connect
with these, I don't think . . .

MAITLAND Isn't it worth just running every name on these
card indexes through the computer . . . ?
Something might come up.

MORSE It's too late.

MAITLAND Not if we start now. There are two machines.
I'll go on this one, you go on that one.

She has stood up and is carrying the Roladexes towards the terminals.

MORSE Come on, we've done enough.

MAITLAND Shame on you.

MORSE *(uncomfortable)* No, no, really.

He's loitering by the terminal, writing his name on the keys, with two fingers. MAITLAND twigs.

MAITLAND Chief Inspector Morse, are you telling me you
don't know how to work the machine?

MORSE I don't know how to work the machine.

MAITLAND Well, sit down, and I'll show you.

MORSE Can we go and get the tape-recorder from
Jackie's flat? I can't think without music.

MAITLAND *(laughing)* Spend a night with a man: it's very
revealing!

74   Interior. Jackie Thorn building. Incident room. Dawn. 74

The room is filling with natural light. The tape-recorder fills it with Vivaldi. The birds have begun their dawn chorus. MORSE and MAITLAND beaver away at the machines. Punching up names, rejecting them.

MAITLAND *(as she taps into the keyboard)* If I hear this piece
of music one more time I'm going to scream.
*(she stops the furious typing and looks at her
watch)* You know it's the morning? This was a
terrible idea of yours.

MORSE　Quite impressive, these machines. Do they take hard disks and things?

MAITLAND　*(cheerful)* Shut up. One minute you don't know how to turn the things on, the next you're a computer bore.

MORSE　Story of my life.

She's typed in a new name. The machine clicks and whirrs.

MORSE　*(cont.)* Okay, so show me how to turn it off.

MAITLAND　*(rising excitement)* I think, I think we're in business! I think we are about to be in business! *(to the machine)* Thank you, thank you, thank you, you little darling!
(she kisses the screen)

MORSE　What?

He stumbles over.

MAITLAND　Philippa Jane Lau. Eurasian.

MORSE　And?

MAITLAND　Philippa Lau was the victim of violent assault

. . .
(calculating madly as she stares at the information) . . . 19 uh — what's that? Five years ago. She was seriously injured. But she survived. She's alive!

MORSE walks over to look at the computer screen. They look at the precious details punched up on the screen.

MAITLAND　*(cont.)* *(holding up an oil-stained service card)* Three months after buying a car from Boynton's garage.

MORSE　Well.

MAITLAND　*(now as convinced as MORSE about Boynton's guilt)* Two's company, Mr Boynton. Three is a crowd!

75   Interior. Jackie Thorn building. Incident room. Morning.

LEWIS is first in this morning. MAITLAND and MORSE have long gone, but their trail is evident, with the pizza container, the beer bottles, the printouts still scattered. LEWIS, pondering, begins to gather them up.

During his domestic duties he notices a large message on his desk. It reads: 'Find out anything you can about the Philippa Lau case. In later. "M".' Pinned to the message is the printout of the information we last saw on the computer screen.

76   Interior. Philippa Lau flat. Hall. Morning.   76

The doorbell rings. PHILIPPA comes apprehensively to the door. Locked and chained as before. She looks in the spyhole. It's MORSE. As far as she is concerned it's another strange man. She doesn't answer. The doorbell rings again.

    MORSE *(outside)* Miss Lau?

She doesn't answer. Silently, she backs down the hall, transfixed.

77   Interior. Jackie Thorn building. Incident room. Morning.   77

LEWIS is now at his desk, the other OFFICERS at work alongside him. There are fewer of them now as the day of the crime recedes and leads diminish. Nobody's on the telephone. DEARDEN walks over with a fax and puts it on Lewis's desk. He's reading it as MAITLAND arrives, breezy, high, a change of clothes. She puts down her bags, walks over to LEWIS, nodding to or greeting her other COLLEAGUES.

    MAITLAND Hi, how are you?

        LEWIS *(terse)* Not so bad, thanks. You?

MAITLAND *(exuberant)* Terrific. Listen, I'm sorry about last night, but it was worth it. Really. Is he in?

LEWIS No. What time did you get finished?

MAITLAND Uh, quite late. Did you get the message?

LEWIS Yes. What was I supposed to be finding out?

MAITLAND Well, Philippa Lau — we think — is another victim. Didn't we leave you the printout?

LEWIS No, she isn't.

MAITLAND How do you know?

LEWIS *(curt)* You're both as bad as each other, aren't you?

MAITLAND What do you mean?

LEWIS *(close to erupting)* In this country, the law says we're innocent until proved guilty. You've already put Jeremy Boynton behind bars, before you even, I mean, if he had died yesterday because of what we'd led Tim Ablett to believe, whose fault would that have been?

MAITLAND Wait a minute, I think —

LEWIS *(cutting her off)* No, you wait a minute — I've had the lab reports this morning: yeah, Boynton was the father of Jackie Thorn's baby, no, he didn't . . . it wasn't rape. She'd had intercourse several hours before she died. You know. Philippa Lau, the man who assaulted her, he's in prison, Sergeant, he was caught and convicted. It had nothing to do with Jeremy Boynton. None of it has. But there's no procedure, there's no, it's crime solved like a crossword puzzle. And I'm sick of it.

The room has gone silent. LEWIS is suddenly aware that this outburst has been overheard by the whole room.

69

LEWIS *(cont.)* Anyway, I'm sorry, but that's how I feel. So.

He looks down at his papers, reddening. MAITLAND goes back to her desk, sits down.

LEWIS *(cont.) (glaring round the room)* Well?

Heads return to their papers.

78   Exterior. Philippa Lau building. Day.   78

MORSE emerges from the building and gets back into the Jag. Turns the key in the ignition. The engine starts. There is a short pop and then smoke starts to appear from under the bonnet.

MORSE Brilliant.

MORSE gets out of the car quickly.

79   Exterior. Street. A little later.   79

The beloved Jag bumps off down the street courtesy of George's trailer. MORSE and LEWIS watch it.

LEWIS Fancy a drink, sir?

MORSE What's the matter?

LEWIS I'm just asking if you want a drink . . .

MORSE Well, something's the matter. How many years have I known you – you don't often ask me to go for a drink.

LEWIS I'm asking now.

MORSE All right. Strangely enough, I know quite a decent hostelry but a few minutes' drive from here.

They walk. MORSE pulls up short, looking at his watch.

MORSE   *(disgruntled)* No, wait a minute, I can't, can I? I've got a driving lesson. And I've paid for it. You couldn't give me a lift? We can chat in the car.
(they're by the door to the Lau building) That's where the Lau woman lives. She wouldn't open the door.

LEWIS sighs.

LEWIS   Yeah, well, you probably scared the living daylights out of her.

MORSE   What?

LEWIS   *(as they reach the car)* Philippa Lau. Did you not think about that? She'll be terrified. Ach! You just trample around, don't you? You're supposed to be so clever, but sometimes I think you're a bloody fool.

MORSE   Lewis, calm down, and tell me what's eating you?

LEWIS   *(opening the car door)* Why didn't you wait and read the case notes? Before you go stirring up the past.
(hands him a buff folder) If you can't be bothered to read the whole lot, just turn to the last page. It's a signed confession.

MORSE gives LEWIS a look, then starts pulling out the papers.

80   Exterior. Driving school. Day.   80

MORSE and LEWIS are arriving in Lewis's car.

MORSE   *(attempting to break the mood)* I could tell you a lot about your driving already, Lewis. Lot of problems.

LEWIS   You're not taking this seriously, are you?

MORSE I am. Yes, I am. My case is falling to pieces . . . my car is falling to pieces, I can't have a drink. And my sergeant wants a transfer. Yes, I'm taking it seriously.

LEWIS I don't want a transfer, I just think perhaps it would be, I don't know.

MORSE Anyway, you might as well know I'm not accepting any of it. Except maybe the drink. I'm not accepting any of it.

LEWIS *(incredulous at MORSE's stubbornness)* Sir, there's a man in prison. Gerry Firth.

MORSE I think we pay him a visit . . .

LEWIS Sir, he's more than a hundred miles away.

MORSE Well, he can't come to us.

WHITTAKER has seen them drive up. He comes out of his office as LEWIS and MORSE are talking.

MORSE *(cont.)* Hello, Derek.

WHITTAKER All well?

MORSE Fine.

WHITTAKER *(cheerfully)* Sergeant.

LEWIS Derek.

MORSE starts to move off with WHITTAKER.

LEWIS So what am I doing?

MORSE holds the file.

MORSE I want to meet this man and get Maitland to call Philippa Lau. It might be better coming from a woman. Derek, you won't mind . . . *(to WHITTAKER)* . . . you won't mind, Derek, if Sergeant Lewis uses your phone?

WHITTAKER No, use the one in my office, my shed, you have to dial 9 for an outside line.

MORSE *(casually)* See you in an hour or two.

LEWIS *(frowning as the two men walk away)* Great.

WHITTAKER *(registering this)* I'll wipe the smile off his face, Sergeant, we're off to the skid-pan. Did you have a good breakfast?

81 Exterior. Residential street. Oxford. Early evening. 81

PAULA parks her Beetle outside the new flat. She lugs out some wallpaper sample books and some material swatches, heads towards the house.

We watch this activity through a windscreen. We hear the eerie melody of the woman singing her torch song.

The red glow of the car clock. A hand reaching into the glove compartment, pulling out the brown carpet tape. And then the knife.

82 Interior. Prison block. Afternoon. 82

A PRISON OFFICER unlocks the door and ushers in MORSE and LEWIS. It's not a cell, but a room set aside for education classes. It's shabby and randomly furnished. This is a different world and in the middle of it sits GERRY FIRTH, a nervous fox of a man in his forties, tattoos showing.

OFFICER *(in the doorway)* All right, Gerry, look a bit lively, son.

FIRTH doesn't look up.

OFFICER Don't let him cadge any cigs off you. *(snaps a smile at LEWIS)* I'll be outside.

> LEWIS Thanks.

And the door clangs shut and is mightily locked.

MORSE and LEWIS sit at the table opposite FIRTH. Again, they adopt a quiet, infinitely reasonable tone. They could be doing a newspaper interview with a minor celebrity.

> LEWIS How are you, Gerry?
>
> FIRTH Yeah, okay.
>
> LEWIS Treating you all right, are they?
>
> FIRTH Yeah.
>
> LEWIS How long you got left?
>
> FIRTH *(suspicious)* A bit.
>
> LEWIS We just had a couple of questions about your sentence. Can we have a little chat?

FIRTH is silent.

> MORSE Or are you not in the mood?
>
> FIRTH I'm not really in the mood.
>
> MORSE Fair enough.

He digs into his waistband and produces a slightly crumpled pack of cigarettes.

> MORSE *(cont.)* *(to LEWIS)* Sergeant?

LEWIS repeats the manoeuvre. They place both packs on the table in front of FIRTH.

> MORSE *(cont.)* Philippa Lau was asking after you.
>
> FIRTH Who?

He reaches towards the cigarettes. MORSE picks them up.

> MORSE Philippa Lau. Have you forgotten her?
> *(to LEWIS)* He can't have forgotten her, can he?

LEWIS I wouldn't have thought so. Philippa Lau — you attacked her, Gerry, you went down for her. She was one of your TICs. We've got your signed statement.
(opens up the file)

FIRTH *(a fox)* Yeah, right.

LEWIS He does remember.

FIRTH Yeah.

MORSE pushes the cigarettes towards him.

MORSE So tell us.

83   Interior. Paula's new flat. Early evening.   83

PAULA is on the floor in the front room. She's taped cloth swatches on the wall, is surrounded by the wallpaper samples. She has a Walkman on and is nodding to its hidden beat. The doorbell rings. She doesn't hear it. It rings again. She slips off the headphones. She's surprised. She's not sure if it really was the door. She walks a little nervously to the door where in the opaque glass the shape of a man is outlined. She pulls the dog-chain across, opens the door.

PAULA Who is it?

MAN *(outside)* Paula?

PAULA *(peering round the gap)* Yes?

Then she sees who's there, and relaxes a little, although still surprised.

PAULA *(cont.) (not familiar — it's been a long time)* Oh, hello.

84   Interior. Jackie Thorn building. Incident room. Early evening.   84

MORSE and LEWIS come into the room. A FEW OFFICERS, MAITLAND and DEARDEN among them, are still working.

DEARDEN (*jumping up anxiously*) Sir, uh, the Super's waiting in your room. He's been an hour. He's not very happy.

MORSE Okay. Anything anybody?

Shrugs and shakes of head. MAITLAND comes over.

MAITLAND Hi.

MORSE Did you get through to her?

MAITLAND Yeah. She's in a pretty bad way.

MORSE Well, I think that's my fault. Isn't that right, Lewis?

LEWIS Well.

MAITLAND Not entirely, sir. I wasn't the only person to telephone this afternoon.

MORSE Oh?

MAITLAND At about four o'clock a man called and, well I've written down what he said as accurately as she could remember.

She goes over to her desk and picks up a piece of paper. STRANGE enters.

STRANGE (*terrifyingly reasonable*) Morse, if you could spare me a few minutes I'd be very grateful.

MORSE (*collecting the sheet from MAITLAND*) Sir.

STRANGE turns and exits, MORSE follows. LEWIS looks at the others.

MORSE heads towards his room.

STRANGE   Not that way. We're going out. I'm taking you for a drink.

MORSE   It's funny, you're the second person to say that to me today. I turned the first one down.

STRANGE   This one you'll need.

85   Interior. Pub. Early evening.   85

STRANGE navigates the crowded bar to where MORSE is sitting reading the message from Maitland. STRANGE has a pint in each hand and passes one to MORSE.

STRANGE   *(as they grasp their pints)* Cheers.

MORSE   *(raising his glass)* Cheers.

They both take a long sup.

STRANGE   *(not aggressively)* You're off this case, mate.

MORSE   Ah.

STRANGE   I spoke to the Deputy CC, and he agrees.

MORSE doesn't respond. He takes another shot of his pint.

STRANGE   That garage business yesterday was the last straw. Boynton could have died, that would have been it for you. I'm not going to even mention the rest of it — papers disappearing overnight without a warrant . . .

MORSE   Give me twenty-four hours.

STRANGE   You're off. You're on leave. Don't make me throw my weight around.

MORSE   Does the name Philippa Lau mean anything to you?

STRANGE   I've heard about that, too. That case was closed, it's five years ago. Get a grip, eh, come on.

MORSE hands him the sheet of paper.

>MORSE   Read that.

>STRANGE *(he reads it aloud – without expression – quite*
>   *fast)* 'Philippa, I'm watching you. Not such a
>   little tease these days are we? Bit harder for a
>   cripple. Whatever you think you remember,
>   forget, forget. I'm watching you and if you start
>   shooting your cheap little mouth off, next time
>   I'll do the job properly.' Well, what's this
>   supposed to be?

>MORSE   It's the transcript of a telephone call Philippa
>   Lau had this afternoon. Now I was at a prison
>   this afternoon talking to the man who's inside
>   for assaulting her. Quite interesting, eh?

>STRANGE *(not showing if he is unsettled)* Doesn't mean
>   anything. He could have had a friend call her, it
>   could be a hoax. That's not evidence.

>MORSE   No. Gerry Firth – he's the con – there was a
>   deal, we did a deal, not we, Nev Batten, but
>   anyway a deal was done, he took on a couple
>   of TICs to clear the books and we put in a
>   good word. Firth knew nothing about her. He
>   didn't know if she was white, black, big, small,
>   fat, thin, old, young, or where she lived or what
>   was done to her. It was a trade-off, sir. And the
>   man who did do it is out there.

>STRANGE *(taking notice now)* And you think it has to be
>   Boynton . . . ?

>MORSE   Philippa Lau bought a car from him. Maureen
>   Thompson the same. Jackie Thorn has an affair
>   with him.
>   *(pleading)* Let me take him into custody. I'm
>   getting the evidence.

STRANGE I don't know.
          (reflecting on the folly of the TIC scam) Nev
          Batten, he never was much of a . . . ach! Bloody
          fool! Well, I don't know, I still think —

We don't find out what STRANGE thinks because an agitated
LEWIS has rushed into the pub and is pushing his way towards
them.

    LEWIS Excuse me, sir. You better come, sir.

    MORSE What?

    LEWIS There's been another killing.

    MORSE *(to STRANGE — exasperated)* Well now will you let
           me pick him up?

    LEWIS It wasn't Jeremy Boynton, sir. They kept him in,
           he's still in the hospital.

MORSE is completely thrown.

86   Interior. Paula's new flat. Night.   86

MORSE is covering up the corpse of PAULA. LEWIS and MAITLAND
are also there. MAITLAND is weeping. Around them the
buzz-buzz of forensic activity. A siren light from outside sends
a revolving blue cast into the room.

MORSE gets up, tries to console MAITLAND.

       MORSE *(soothing)* Hey . . .

   MAITLAND This is not very professional, I know.

      MORSE I feel the same.

   MAITLAND We should have caught this man. We should
             have caught this man before this.

      LEWIS *(not harshly — but this is the nadir)* Just for the
             record, sir, Paula Steadman does not and never
             has owned a car from Boynton's Garage.

MORSE stands opposite the Boynton Garage, adjacent to the driving school entrance. Traffic goes by. You get the impression he's been there a long time, sniffing the air. His expression is blank, drawn.

KASS sees him and closes the blind.

LEWIS is laying out photographs along the table. The victims, the families and friends of the victims. So we'll recognise Ablett and Mrs Thorn alongside Jackie, plus Boynton. Paula's friend Rachel in that group, etc.

> LEWIS Anyone you recognise here?

PHILIPPA looks closely, picks up Jackie's picture.

> PHILIPPA Was this woman killed?

> MAITLAND Yeah.

> PHILIPPA Who's this?

> MAITLAND Her mother.

> PHILIPPA God.
> *(keeps looking)* No, I'm sorry. I've never seen any of these people before.

> LEWIS Do you remember anything about your attack? I've seen the file and you were — I expect it was the shock — but I know you said then you couldn't remember anything.

> PHILIPPA I have dreams. I have these dreams about him. And I see his face. But I couldn't describe him. And he changes anyway, so . . .

89   Exterior. Driving course track. Morning.   89

Whittaker's car speeds along the course. MORSE is driving. Tyres and cones require MORSE to negotiate at speed.

WHITTAKER What we're aiming for is developing some foresight.

MORSE I could do with some of that.

WHITTAKER I drive up the motorway every evening and I don't want to touch the brakes at all if I can help it.

MORSE I thought you lived in Oxford?

WHITTAKER I do.

MORSE Why do you use the motorway?

WHITTAKER *(tight)* My wife's in a, she had a stroke and she's in a clinic, so I go up to visit her.

MORSE I'm sorry.

WHITTAKER Yeah.

MORSE Is this recent?

WHITTAKER Couple of months. It happened before, a few years back, but I got her home. They don't think she's going to be able to . . . Doesn't know who I am. That's why I've got no time for the likes of Boynton.
(suddenly poisonous) Running after any tart in a tight skirt.

MORSE, miscalculating, takes a bend too fast and hits a pile of cones, sending them flying across the track.

90   Interior. Philippa Lau flat. Hall. Morning.   90

LEWIS, MAITLAND and PHILIPPA are at the door, staring at the safety measures, the locks and chains and infra-red.

MAITLAND   Can I come back? Could I come back and see
you?

PHILIPPA   You don't have to.

LEWIS   *(in the doorway)* So when you got your car,
when you got it from Boynton's, was it the
sales manager there who sold it or who?

PHILIPPA   No. I didn't buy it myself. It was bought for me,
I mean, I paid for it, but —

LEWIS   What? You mean your brother?

PHILIPPA   *(ruefully to* MAITLAND — *whom she likes very
much)* No, I know this sounds a bit pathetic, but
I was very nervous about driving. It took me a
long time to pass my test and so I went to this
place, a centre, where you can, they've got like
these video machines and a pretend road
system, and —

LEWIS and MAITLAND, their minds racing.

91   Exterior. Whittaker's car. Morning.   91

PHILIPPA   *(voice-over)* — my instructor, who was very, he
was nice and obviously knew a lot about cars,
and he, actually he just got me the same car I
was learning in.

MORSE and his very nice INSTRUCTOR speed around the course.

WHITTAKER   *(writing on the clipboard)* Good. We're making a
halfway decent driver out of you.
(his biro gives up on him) Blasted thing.

He hunts around for another pen in his jacket, can't find one.

He opens up the glove compartment. From under a roll of
brown tape he produces a clutch of biros. MORSE glances across.

Sees the tape. Back to his driving. Frowns.

> MORSE I do like this car.

> WHITTAKER It's all right.

> MORSE I suppose it's um . . . you get used to learning on something and um . . .

> WHITTAKER Right.

> MORSE That's what you were saying about a lot of your learners buying the same car.

> WHITTAKER Oh yes, Boynton's have done very well out of us.

The sound of a siren can be heard. Cut to LEWIS and MAITLAND who are speeding through the streets.

> MORSE Did Maureen Thompson buy one?

> WHITTAKER I think she did, yes.

> MORSE And Jackie Thorn?

> WHITTAKER Very clever, very clever, Inspector Morse. Yes, yes, she bought her car. They all did. Whores, little bitches on heat.

> MORSE Yes, I know just what you mean Derek. I know exactly what you mean. They ask for it.

> WHITTAKER They used to sit in my car half-naked. They're daughters of Satan, and there's my wife who's a saint. I'm not kidding. I'm afraid I've got to keep you quiet, Inspector Morse – sorry.

WHITTAKER leans across to the glove compartment, releasing his seat belt just as MORSE drives through the sprinkler section of the course. Suddenly they're in the equivalent of a storm. MORSE can't find the wipers. He can't see. He's panicking.

WHITTAKER's got the knife and he's lunging at MORSE. And an almighty struggle breaks out, with MORSE trying to fend off the knife and WHITTAKER, literally a man possessed, climbing out of his seat. The car veers wildly from side to side on the banked bend. Then they're soaring up and over the humpback bridge, to arrive at the other side just as LEWIS and MAITLAND drive across the T-junction at right-angles to them. MORSE loses control and the car goes into a skid.

WHITTAKER is thrown back. MORSE remembers his lessons and steers into the skid. He somehow misses LEWIS and MAITLAND and brings the car smashing sideways against the nearside lane on the passenger side, sending tyres spiralling across the track.

LEWIS and MAITLAND find MORSE head bowed, still in the driver's seat. He's got a wound or two in his arm and is bleeding. WHITTAKER is slumped forward. LEWIS pulls him back. The knife is forced up into his heart.

MAITLAND Sir?

MORSE *(shaken up)* I'm fine.
(trying to shrug it off) I've had lessons on the skid-pan.
(to LEWIS) Hello.
(he's about to crack) It sounds stupid, but I can't get my hands off the wheel.

MAITLAND gently uncurls his fingers.

92   Interior. Hospital. Side room. Day.   92

MORSE has one arm in a sling, and he's carrying a steering wheel in the other. He sees BOYNTON, who has been discharged and is packing his belongings.

MORSE I owe you an apology.

BOYNTON Yes.

MORSE I couldn't see the wood for the trees. Not for the first time. Did you hear what happened?

BOYNTON Sergeant Lewis came down.

MORSE And you're off home?

BOYNTON Yep.

MORSE *(handing him the steering wheel)* Peace offering.

BOYNTON What is this?

MORSE I've had this for years. I got it at some auction or other. It won the Monte Carlo rally in 1956. Not by itself, of course . . . I've never had the car to put it in. I think you do. And I'm sorry. Anyway.

BOYNTON How's your arm?

MORSE Sore.

BOYNTON You deserve it.

MORSE *(sour)* Thanks.

93 Interior. Jackie Thorn building. Incident room. Morning. 93

The incident room is in a state of deconstruction. MAITLAND is filling up a large holdall with her belongings. LEWIS, DEARDEN and a FEW OTHERS do the same. MAITLAND walks out of the room.

94 Interior. Jackie Thorn building. Incident centre. Morse's room. Morning. 94

MORSE is also clearing away, sling abandoned and hanging ludicrously as he carries boxes. MAITLAND walks in.

MAITLAND 'Bye.

MORSE 'Bye.

MAITLAND I thought you weren't meant to be carrying stuff?

MORSE *(shrugs)* Well, tell me not to do something and I, well, you know.

MAITLAND So if I ask you not to keep in touch?

MORSE looks a bit sad. It's only a gesture and he knows it.

MORSE Thanks, Siobhan.

MAITLAND I'll see you.

They shake hands affectionately.

95   Exterior. Open road. Day.   95

MORSE is driving the Jag through Oxford. The Morse theme plays. The CREDITS ROLL.

End of Act Four

END

Notes

This particular episode of *Morse* follows the easily recognisable format established by earlier films. Set in Oxford, the pace is slow, the emphasis is on the character of Morse and the further development of his personality and relationships, the themes are powerful and strongly interrelated, and the images are lush.

Driven to Distraction begins, appropriately enough, with Morse and Lewis stuck in a traffic jam. Morse is frustrated by the delay and finds it hard to control his impatience. This opening scene introduces some of the more important themes dealt with in this episode. Jackie Thorn, the second murder victim, is in the car in front. She seems preoccupied and is obviously having a bad day. A music cassette has spilled its tape all over her car and she is desperately trying to sort out the mess. As the line of cars moves, Morse sounds his horn to make her hurry. This startles and upsets her. This action on Morse's part immediately puts him in the role of aggressor and makes Jackie Thorn appear vulnerable; a victim of Morse's rude, assertive behaviour. The tape also links Morse to the murder as it is later seen wrapped around the feet of her killer as he leaves her apartment. We are witness to the beginnings of what becomes an ongoing debate between Morse and Lewis on the nature of policing and the way the force relates to and is viewed by the community. Morse has no qualms about the misuse of his authority and would quite happily put on the car's siren in order to retrieve his car from the garage. Lewis makes his disapproval obvious, thinking Morse both irresponsible and insensitive. Much of the scene is shot from the interior of the two cars. Cars, as images and metaphors, are central to this episode. Much of the filming is from the interior of cars looking out and most of the important scenes and conversations take place inside cars.

Cars offer directors the opportunity to make use of enclosed spaces. This can cause an atmosphere of intimacy or entrapment. The cars in this episode allow the characters to reveal themselves, their ideas and opinions. Maitland uses her car in an attempt to show Morse and Lewis how vulnerable women alone are (although at this stage only Lewis allows himself to become more aware and sensitive to the issue). At the beginning of Act 2, scene 23, Maitland and Morse begin to forge a more positive relationship within the closeness of Morse's car – helped by their mutual appreciation of Bach. Boynton's threatening behaviour towards Angie Howe is made much more menacing by the enclosed environment of his car. Morse talks to Whittaker and puts himself in a very vulnerable position within the confines of Whittaker's car. In the final, climactic scene Morse is trapped with Whittaker in a car he cannot control.

Cars are also used as a device to blur our understanding of the plot. We, like Morse, are prevented from solving the crime and recognising the murderer. The murder victims are viewed from within the murderer's car. He follows them like a predator stalking prey. The camera focuses on the dashboard: the gloved hands on the steering wheel, the lit-up displays; the same song is repeated. The viewer is placed with the murderer firmly in the position of voyeur, and it is very disturbing. But our judgement, like Morse's, becomes confused. In scene 8, Boynton's car is mistaken by us for the murderer's by the way it is filmed. He becomes for us, as well as Morse, the prime suspect.

Both Boynton, the main suspect, and Whittaker, the murderer, work with cars. Jeremy Boynton sells them and Derek Whittaker teaches people to drive them. Morse is firmly associated in our minds with his polished red Jaguar. Appreciating and enjoying cars is traditionally a male occupation: 'Everyone knows cars have got nothing to do with women' (scene 31). Boynton lists his collection of classic Jags with pride, hoping to impress a fellow male – Morse. It is Whittaker who explains, 'Goes together, apparently, love of beautiful cars, love of the ladies. And you say you have a Jaguar yourself?' (scene 35). But we learn early on that although Morse takes pride in the aesthetics of motoring, he does not look after his car and is loath to spend any money on it. This is something he has in common with Maitland: '. . . there are things growing and crawling about in mine' (scene 23).

The important male protagonists are all first seen in cars. Whittaker and Boynton are linked by their car-related professions. Both as car salesman and driving instructor they are brought into contact with the public, and more specifically the murder victims.

Morse, although he takes a snobbish pride in his car, cannot claim to be a good driver ('You're not so bad. We'll make a driver out of you yet', scene 66), or a careful owner ('Needs a little love and attention, if you don't mind me saying so . . .', scene 27). Because of this Morse has put himself in the traditionally female role in relation to cars. He seeks instruction from Derek Whittaker, as do the murder victims and Mrs Lewis, and consequently he becomes Whittaker's last intended victim. It is interesting that despite this, Morse uses his red Jaguar as a representative of himself when he parks it on Boynton's forecourt as a means of intimidation. He does this ironically enough in order to lean on Boynton. But by walking around the corner to take driving lessons with Whittaker he is inadvertently putting the guilty man under massive pressure.

This episode of *Morse* is very much about men: their relationships with and attitudes to women, and the causes of violent crime towards women. Morse, Lewis, Boynton, Whittaker and Tim Ablett are the men at the centre of this murder inquiry. Morse finds he dislikes Boynton instantly but they do have some character traits in common. Boynton jocularly says to Morse, [you're] 'a man after my own heart, Inspector' (scene 38) – hardly a compliment in Morse's eyes. Morse enjoys his ownership of the Jag while Boynton ostentatiously owns a fleet. Morse is sexist; he judges women by their appearance. Many of the problems in his relationships with women are due to the narrow way in which he perceives them. Boynton takes sexism to new heights. He uses women in a cold, ruthless way which Morse finds himself thoroughly disapproving of. Kass is presented as an apprentice Boynton. He is smug and self-satisfied and has made a less successful play for Jackie Thorn. Morse is a gentleman of the 'old school': women are considered different, they are there to be admired, cosseted and cared for but are beings incapable of being understood. Boynton views things very differently. He is unfaithful to his wife and she obviously suspects him; it is suggested that he has been violent towards his first wife, and when Jackie Thorn dies we are shown no remorse, guilt or sadness. The concept of self is at the centre of all his relationships. (It is interesting to reflect here on the meal Jackie was planning with Boynton. The pains she had taken with the flowers, the wine and the cigar all suggest she was going to tell him of her pregnancy. Did she wish him to leave his wife and if so, how would he have responded?) When Morse begins to put pressure on Boynton, he is very aggressive and threatening. Boynton, when phoning his solicitor, calls Morse 'a little bully-boy' (scene 67). Yet these are exactly the tactics he makes use of in relation to Angie Howe. It is a stereotypically male way of dealing with the world – imposing your will at all costs, the end results justifying the means.

Morse is, in many ways, a very sensitive man. He abhors violence and finds it hard to deal with the victims and their relatives. When faced with the scene of destruction at Jackie Thorn's flat he copes by becoming light-hearted. He deals with the death of Paula Steadman much more thoughtfully. Morse is introspective and desirous of becoming a better man. He is capable of learning from his mistakes and his clumsiness. We are never given the impression that Boynton would acknowledge or act upon any such self-doubt. In contrast to Boynton, Tim Ablett is distraught at the death of Jackie. His character shows a vulnerability and innocence which Morse shares, but Boynton does not. Ablett obviously loves Jackie Thorn, but shows a real lack of understanding about her character and certain aspects of her life. He does not cope well with the practicalities of life on his own. His house is a tip, and he dyes all his washing pink at the launderette. It seems that Jackie used to do this for him. But he too, when angry and frustrated resorts to violence, threatening Boynton in his office and attacking him on his forecourt: behaviour reminiscent of both Morse and Boynton.

Morse sympathises with Tim Ablett. He understands him and his pain. When apologising for his behaviour at the scene of Jackie's death Tim accepts it fully. Boynton, however, is presented unsympathetically to the end. He does not acknowledge Morse's apology and appears to relish his discomfort just as Morse has done with him in earlier scenes. Whittaker is the ultimate predatory male. His manner changes completely when he realises Morse knows the truth; the façade has dropped. There is some justice in the fact that he is killed with his own murder weapon in the car he has used to stalk his prey. Boynton may be bent on ruthless self-preservation, but Whittaker proves to be insane in a manic, religious way. He disapproves of Boynton's womanising and finds himself unable to come to terms with women who are independent and behave in a way he perceives as sexual. He calls his victims 'whores, little bitches on heat' (scene 91). The killings link directly to his feelings of bitterness and frustration caused by his wife's two strokes: 'They're daughters of Satan, and there's my wife who's a saint' (scene 91). He is himself a victim of circumstance and his own warped psychology. Whittaker is the extreme result of a male dominated, sexist world.

After a bad start, Sergeant Maitland's relationship with Morse develops steadily. Morse is initially very suspicious of Maitland. He does not find her manner attractive and he distrusts her as a colleague. When Maitland addresses the force about the case, Morse marks her down as a theorist – someone who relies on rigid method rather than intuition and instinct. Morse is constantly being brought to task for his unorthodox methods. He has to defend himself to Strange when questioned about his lack of firm evidence: '. . . it'll fall into place . . . we've both been at this too long, you get an instinct' (scene 53); 'Let me take him into custody. I'm getting the evidence' (scene 85). At first Morse does not allow himself to learn anything from Maitland. But she is intelligent and an intellectual. Morse admires and values intellect. This is something Lewis does not possess. Maitland also proves to be a good practical police officer: it is she who makes the initial link between the murder victims and the cars. Morse finds he has much to learn from her – professionally about crimes of violence against women and more personally about how to work fruitfully and respectfully with a colleague of the opposite sex. It is she and not Lewis who agrees that ransacking Boynton's office is the right thing to do. They reach a new degree of closeness as they work through the night, both driven by a certain obsessiveness in their natures. They also make the same mistake in pursuing Boynton so narrow-mindedly, both motivated by strong personal dislike of him. The emphasis on instinct over method leaves Morse in a vulnerable situation at the end, having to improvise desperately to save his own life. Lewis with his more careful and thorough methods manages to come to the same conclusion but with less dramatic consequences.

Lewis at one point during this episode considers asking for a transfer. He is a man of principle, and although he reveres Morse and often lacks confidence, he is willing to make a stand on a point of conscience. In this way Lewis is as enigmatic a character as Morse. We hear a great deal about Val and the children, but we see almost nothing of his home life. The relationship between these two very different men is one of the central points of interest in any Morse story. (In some ways this is less the case in this episode than many others – Morse's relationship with Maitland takes centre stage in order to portray the complexities of developing a successful platonic but caring professional male/female relationship.) Is Lewis presented as being envious in any way? On the surface Maitland has far more in common with Morse than Lewis does.

Driven to Distraction ends with Whittaker – the killer – dead. But there is no evidence that Boynton has been softened by his experiences. His final conversation with Morse has him answering curtly and bitterly. Morse knows his own weaknesses: 'I couldn't see the wood for the trees. Not for the first time' (scene 92). Boynton refuses to bend at all. The man has no sense of self or sense of humour:

BOYNTON How's your arm?

  MORSE Sore.

BOYNTON You deserve it.

  MORSE *(sour)* Thanks.

This scene is played with no tone of irony on Boynton's part at all. We are left to assume that he, along with his brand of sexism, will continue much as before. But Morse has learned a lot from the case. Apart from the influences of Maitland he has achieved the ultimate learning experience by being placed in the role of victim. Although the tone of the final scenes are of sadness, we are left on the more positive note of a world which is adapting – slowly and painfully to be sure – but nevertheless changing for the better.

Further reading and watching

Edgar Allan Poe	*The Murders in the Rue Morgue* (1841)
Charles Dickens	*Bleak House* (1853)
	The Mystery of Edwin Drood (1870)
Wilkie Collins	*Woman in White* (1860)
	The Moonstone (1868)
Arthur Conan Doyle	*The Hound of the Baskervilles* (1902)
	The Return of Sherlock Holmes (a collection of short stories, 1905)
Margery Allingham	*Flowers for the Judge* (1936)
	The Tiger in the Smoke (1952)
Agatha Christie	*The Mirror Cracked from Side to Side* (1960)
	Death on the Nile (1937)
Raymond Chandler	*The Big Sleep* (1939)
	The High Window (1942)
P. D. James	*An Unsuitable Job for a Woman* (1972)
	A Taste for Death (1988)
	Devices and Desires (1989)
Ellis Peters	*A Morbid Taste for Bones* (1977)
	The Confession of Brother Halvin (1987)
Umberto Eco	*The Name of the Rose* (1980)
Colin Dexter	*The Wench is Dead* (1989)
	The Way Through the Woods (1992)

Teaching *Driven to Distraction*

Driven to Distraction can be taught as a television film with the script as a study aid, or by using the script as the primary source. It fits neatly into most Language and Literature syllabuses, either as a literature text, covering the media element, or as a language assignment. It also has all the qualities needed to make a challenging text for any media studies course.

The first need is for the film to be shown and for the students to be given the chance to discuss and write down their impressions. Certain scenes – the first, for example – need to be studied in depth. It is important that central characters, themes and images are traced through. The film needs to be paused so that students can study characters' responses, facial expressions, body language and clothing, as well as sets, camera angles and repeated visual images and links. Turning off the picture and listening to the voices, sounds and music and then watching without sound are interesting ways to study scenes in this episode.

Allowing students to make their own television gives the most valuable insight into the problems and possibilities of television production. Approaches that work well and are not time-consuming include making a documentary, news broadcast, simple plays, interviews, and 'talking head' monologues. All of these can be linked to *Driven to Distraction.* The monologue could, for example, be Maitland talking about her life, her job and her response to what has happened in this episode. A documentary could deal with one of the issues raised – perhaps crimes against women, methods of policing, or sexism in the world of work.

The following suggestions for assignment titles or discussion starters are not ranked in order of difficulty – it would be impossible to achieve that successfully. They cover a wide range of criteria for Key Stage 4 English, Literature, and Media Studies for GCSE, and are also appropriate for A level coursework for English, Media, and Communications courses.

Assignment titles/Discussion starters

1 Write Sergeant Maitland's official report on the crimes, piecing together the evidence in an ordered way.

2 Write a conversation between Lewis and his wife in which he describes his relationship with Morse. Relate it to this episode in particular.

3 Script the official inquest into the murders and Whittaker's death.

4 Confining yourself solely to the use of music and images, describe how Morse's character is created in this episode.

5 How are people's home environment and clothes used to establish character?

6 What for you are the most memorable images in the film? Why are they so memorable?

7 Write two further scenes (at whatever point you wish).

8 Try to explain why Morse is so popular, and give your personal opinion.

9 Compare Morse with another TV detective (eg Dalgliesh or Wexford).

10 Choose a novel by Colin Dexter that has been adapted for television. Compare the book with the TV version, and say which you find the most effective vehicle. (Possible choices include *The Dead of Jericho*, *The Silent World of Nicholas Quinn*, *Last Seen Wearing*, or *Last Bus to Woodstock*.)

11 Trace the theme of sexism as it is dealt with in this episode.

12 How does the portrayal of the central character in detective fiction and films present a way of looking at the world? Discuss in relation to particular texts.

13 Do you agree that detective fiction tends to be unacceptably sexist?

14 Looking at detective novels written over the last hundred years, what do you notice about their development?